ISRAEL

A Spiritual
Travel Guide
2nd Edition

Other Jewish Lights Books about Israel and Jewish Spirituality

A Dream of Zion
American Jews Reflect on Why Israel Matters to Them
Edited by Rabbi Jeffrey K. Salkin

Women of the Wall
Claiming Sacred Ground at Judaism's Holy Site
Edited by Phyllis Chesler and Rivka Haut

The Jewish Connection to Israel, the Promised Land
A Brief Introduction for Christians
By Rabbi Eugene Korn, PhD

On the Chocolate Trail
*A Delicious Adventure Connecting Jews, Religions, History, Travel,
Rituals and Recipes to the Magic of Cacao*
By Rabbi Deborah R. Prinz

ISRAEL

A Spiritual Travel Guide

2nd Edition

A Companion for the
Modern Jewish Pilgrim

Rabbi Lawrence A. Hoffman, PhD

JEWISH LIGHTS Publishing

Israel—A Spiritual Travel Guide, 2nd Edition:
A Companion for the Modern Jewish Pilgrim

2022 Sixth Printing

Grateful acknowledgment is made for permission to reprint the following materials:

Yehuda Amichai, *Poems of Jerusalem,* New York: Harper & Row, 1996; Lawrence Fine, ed., *Safed Spirituality,* Mahwah, NJ: Paulist Press, 1984; A.D. Gordon, *A.D. Gordon Selected Essays,* North Stratford, NH: Ayer Company, Publishers, Inc., 1938; Danny Siegel, *Before Our Very Eyes: Reading for a Journey Through Israel,* Pittsboro, NC: Town House Press, 1986.

Front cover map: Panoramic Views of the Holy Land by Rabbi H.S. Pinie. Lithography, Turec, 1875. Interior map: Map of the Holy Land by Avraham Bar-Yaakov, 1696. The first Hebrew map of Israel. Both maps courtesy of the National Maritime Museum, Haifa, Israel.

Library of Congress Cataloging-in-Publication Data
Available upon request.
ISBN 978-1-58023-380-4 (eBook)
ISBN-13: 978-1-68442-930-1 (paperback)
10 9 8 7 6

Manufactured in the United States of America
Cover design by Lindy Gifford
Text design by Chelsea Dippel

Published by Jewish Lights Publishing
A Division of LongHill Partners, Inc.
An Imprint of Turner Publishing Company
4507 Charlotte Avenue, Suite 100
Nashville, TN 37209
www.turnerbookstore.com
www.jewishlights.com

In loving memory of
Rabbi Morris N. Kertzer and Dr. Allen A. Small,
lovers of Israel, the People and the Land.

Contents

SECTION ONE

L'chayim! Eighteen Days of Spiritual Preparation
or, What to Do Before You Leave   **13**

Something Better than "Wow!"   **15**

READING ONE: Spiritual Preparation   18

READING TWO: The World Doesn't Really
Look Like That   19

READING THREE: Choosing the Right Map   21

READING FOUR: A Jewish Map for Jewish
Pilgrims   23

READING FIVE: The Jewish Map of Jewish
Space and Time   25

READING SIX: Becoming a Jewish Pilgrim   27

READING SEVEN: Pilgrim or Tourist?   29

READING EIGHT: Sights and Sites   31

READING NINE: Having a Home   33

READING TEN: Returning Home   35

READING ELEVEN: A Pilgrim's Geography:
Out of the Wilderness   36

READING TWELVE: A Pilgrim's Geography:
From the Coastland to the Galil   40

READING THIRTEEN: Jerusalem: The Center
of the World   43

READING FOURTEEN: Where You Know that
You Feel What You Cannot See   45

READING FIFTEEN: What I Learned from
My Grandfather's Watch   47

READING SIXTEEN: Anticipate, Approach,
Acknowledge—and Afterthought   49

READING SEVENTEEN: Blessings!   51

READING EIGHTEEN: A Pilgrim's Diary:
Memories in the Making   53

SECTION TWO

T'fillat Haderekh: **Prayers Before Leaving, for Synagogue and Home**
or, What to Say on the Eve of Leaving

55

For the Shabbat Prior to Leaving

57

SECTION THREE

How to Shape Sacred Time
or, How to Prepare While on the Way

61

A. Finding (and Using) What You Want   63
B. The Jewish Dimension   68
C. The Personal Dimension   69

SECTION FOUR

This Place Is Holy
or, What to Say at Specific Places

81

The Galil: *"Tsafonah*—to the North"

83

Deganya, Kibbutz in the Galil, Or Cemetery
of *Chalutzim* (Pioneers) at the *Kinneret*
(Sea of Galilee)   84

Jezreel Valley   89

Safed   94

The Negev: "*Negbah*—to the South"

99

Dead Sea and Sodom   100

Ein Gedi   104

At a Kibbutz in the Negev 109

Sedeh Boker—David Ben-Gurion's Home 113

Masada 117

Jerusalem and Vicinity: "*Kedmah*—to the East" 121

At the Jaffa Gate 127

In Old Jerusalem 132

Har Herzl 136

At the Knesset 140

The *Kotel* (The Wall) 146

The Temple Mount 149

The Southern Wall to the Temple Mount 153

Mount Scopus 157

The Valleys of Jerusalem 161

Yad Vashem 165

Yemin Moshe (at The Windmill) 171

Mount Nebo 174

Hebron and Bethlehem: Tombs of the
Matriarchs and Patriarchs 179

The Coastal Plain: "*Yamah*—to the West" 183

The Mediterranean 184

Haifa—Mount Carmel 187

Tel Aviv—Beit Hat'futsot (Museum of the
Diaspora) 193

SECTION FIVE

The Guide to Blessing
or, How to Find Blessing Wherever You Go 197

For a Place of Aliyah Such As a *Merkaz
K'litah* (Absorption Center) 199

For a Place of Beauty 200

For a Place of Blessing 201

For a Place of Miracle 202

For a Place of Study   203

On Praying in a Synagogue, New or Old   205

For a Place of Recent Tragedy   207

For a Place of Wisdom   210

For a Place of War   211

For a Place of Hope   212

For a Place of Muslim or Christian Worship   213

For Seeing or Hearing Hebrew All
    around You   213

For Planting a Tree   214

On Eating at a Kibbutz   215

For a Variety of Special Occasions   218

For the Airplane: Prayer for a Safe Journey
    to Israel   221

For the Airplane: Prayer for a Safe Journey
    Home   223

On Waking Up and Going to Bed Each Day   224

SECTION SIX

A Meal in Jerusalem
or, How to Celebrate Like a Pilgrim   **227**

Before Eating   229

After Eating   230

Notes   237

Index of Places and Occasions for Which
    Prayers Are Provided   245

Acknowledgments

This book has been long in the making, and as such, owes a great deal to very many people. Rabbis Eleanor Smith and Adam Stock Spilker (then still student rabbis) were of help in the preliminary stages of my research. Soon-to-be-rabbi Jennifer Krause continued the research, and Adina Hamik worked with me to get the book ready for production.

Thanks should go to several friends and colleagues who read the manuscript at various stages of its evolution. I received valuable advice from Rabbi Rolando Matalon and Rabbi Shira Milgrom. Rabbi Richard Jacobs, Rabbi Kerry Olitzky, and Rabbi Levi Weiman–Kelman read the manuscript from cover to cover, improving it enormously with their insight, and Adina Hamik took a copy with her to Israel, actually trying it out and offering valuable suggestions based on her experience with it. I also thank Joel Hoffman for supplying the translation of the song, "Jerusalem of Gold."

Stuart Matlins, publisher of Jewish Lights, deserves the abiding thanks of his reading public for making available not just this book, but so many others. Jewish Lights Publishing is more than a business for him; it is his consuming passion, a genuine calling, and an everlasting gift to the world of the spirit. Sandra Korinchak, Arthur Magida, and Jennifer Goneau were exceptional editors, to whom I am grateful.

L'chayim!
Eighteen Days of
Spiritual Preparation

or

What to Do Before You Leave

הִנְנִי מוּכָן וּמְזֻמָּן ...

Hin'ni mukhan um'zuman . . .

Here I am, ready and prepared . . .

—*Traditional liturgy*

Something Better than "Wow!"

Everyone remembers that first trip to Israel. When I went there my first time, a veteran traveler remarked, "I envy you. You can visit Israel many times, but you can go there the first time only once." Then he added, "Wait and see. Jerusalem really is just a little bit closer to heaven."

Exactly a week later, I was actually there. The first morning, I wandered the Jerusalem streets, amazed at how modern the place was. Turning the corner, I found myself face to face with antiquity. It was the Old City, its walls rising from the ground like a great geological rift of time buckling up through the centuries. I knew instantly what Moses must have felt when he saw the burning bush.

I had felt it the night before too as, in the dark, our taxi climbed the highway to Jerusalem. How many times had I read the old translation of Psalm 24, "Who shall ascend the mountain of the Lord? Who shall stand in His holy place?" How many pilgrims like myself had ascended this very hill through the centuries? At the side of the road, I thought I made out the shapes of rusted tank remains from the 1948 War of Independence, left there purposely, as symbols of the modern-day miracle of the birth of the state.

I would come to know that feeling many times, sometimes in the most unlikely spots, like picnicking with my children in Ashkelon on an old rock that turned out to be part of a genuine Roman column more than 2,000 years old. My kids were unmoved. "Just more ruins," one of them sighed, completely unimpressed by history. We call such people "cultural philistines," I mused. Then I remembered that once, real Philistines sat here, maybe even Goliath himself. Goliath was long gone now, as were the Romans of old, but the Jewish

People and its faith were still here, still alive and well.

Then there was the time I came across the old cemetery in Safed, with the graves of Judaism's brilliant sixteenth-century mystics. I had sung their songs, read their books, and knew their names as well as my own, but only then did their real presence become tangible to me. Or the sunny afternoon I stood in Jerusalem at King David's grave—whether he was actually buried there or not, his memory was freshly felt for sure.

And here was my problem: When I came across such places, I would just stare in disbelief. All I could find within me was something approaching "Wow!" Sometimes I'd clutch my wife's hand or put my arm around my children, but there was nothing I could say or do to express the religious awe that welled up deep inside my soul.

There must be something better than "Wow!" I thought. And indeed, there was. I had just never considered it. It had never occurred to me to look toward the Jewish tradition for ways to express religious feelings. For my family's stay in Israel I had purchased plane fare, rented an apartment, arranged for the children to attend day camp, and bought canteens. I had done all the things the guidebooks tell you to do, but I had not prepared myself spiritually for the occasion.

Secularism runs so deep that we often reduce spiritual moments to mere lessons in history. We come to Israel prepared for a detached appreciation of battles and monuments: how the great King Herod built the Jerusalem walls, or how sixteenth- and seventeenth-century Ottoman emperors added to them. We are ready to acknowledge the artistic side of Israel too. Guides take time out to admire the Chagalls in the Knesset or the antiquities at the Israel Museum. We are good at history, good at aesthetics, not so good at the life of the spirit.

There must be an easy way for visitors to Israel to do better than "Wow!" when gripped by the feeling that perhaps we are just a little closer to heaven—or that heaven has dropped down a little closer to us. This book provides spiritual preparations for traveling to Israel, and the responses to being there that Jews have practiced since time immemorial.

It combines ancient blessings with medieval prayers, modern poetry, traditional practices, and the opportunity for spiritual reflection, so you can more deeply appreciate the sacred sites and sounds that make Israel the center of the Jewish world.

This is the book I wish I had had when I went to Israel my first time. It gives you a chance to say more than "Wow!"

To let you take it all in, this introduction has been divided into eighteen short readings: eighteen for *chai*, meaning "life." You have a choice: You may spread them out over three weeks, reading one a night for eighteen nights (excluding Shabbat) or you may read six at a time on each of three *Shabbatot*. Nothing better expresses the spirit of Shabbat than preparing to be a pilgrim to the land of our ancestors. The three-week model is borrowed from ancient rabbinic advice on preparing for Passover. Passover was then a pilgrimage event so grand that the Temple had to triple its staff to handle the sacrifices. Roughly three weeks in advance of the holiday a Torah reading advised Jews to begin their ritual preparation for their journey to Jerusalem.

Think of it: this is the land where Abraham and Sarah established Jewish life 4,000 years ago. It is the very same land where, one thousand years later, David and Solomon established the first Jewish commonwealth; the same land where a second Jewish commonwealth arose about a thousand years later; and the land to which we have come back 2,000 years after that.

Whether you cover one reading a day or six on each Shabbat, the main thing is to take three weeks to go through them all. Do not cram the night before you leave. Do not count on reading whenever you get the chance. Do not squeeze the readings into your crowded day, the way you would a newspaper editorial or junk mail that comes to your home. The operative word is *kavvanah*, the rabbinic term for focusing attention on the spiritual challenge of the moment and not letting your mind wander. Your trip can be just another vacation, or it can be the journey of your life. To make it the latter, do it right. Put aside some sacrosanct time, either five minutes for each of eighteen nights or half an hour on three successive *Shabbatot.*

The Kabbalists began their prayers by saying "*Hin'ni mukhan um'zuman,*" "Here I am, ready and prepared." But why both "ready" *and* "prepared"? Why the redundancy? "Ready" means outfitted physically—prayer book in hand, dressed correctly. "Prepared" means outfitted *within,* like an athlete or musician who knows that running shoes and tuned violin strings are only half of what goes into a great performance. The other half is *kavvanah.*

SET 1

READING ONE
Spiritual Preparation

Important moments require preparation. Graduations, for instance, do not just happen. The whole school may know that you have completed all the requirements, but you are still expected to list your name with the registrar, pay off all your debts, maybe rent a gown or cap, and sometimes, even attend rehearsal. Your family and friends, meanwhile, need to know the date, and you may need to make hotel reservations for them. The same is true of weddings, or a bar or bat mitzvah; even a birthday party for your ten-year-old. *Everything* takes preparation.

Journeys take preparation too.

Some of the preparation that goes into a trip is mindless detail: picking up the plane tickets or buying the guidebook. Some of it takes thought: where to go and what book to buy. To be sure, it is possible to show up at an airport and ask for a ticket on the next plane to anywhere. But we would look suspiciously at you if you woke up one day and suddenly left town, notifying no one and ignoring whatever schedule you had already set up. Is it possible? Yes. Is it likely? No.

Busy people find it especially difficult to plan their trips the way they like. Some things almost never get done—like buying a book for the airplane, a task likely to be taken care of only in the airport bookstore. But we do take care of necessary *physical* chores, like picking up our tickets or having them mailed to us. And we engage in required *mental* preparation too: deciding how long to stay and who will stay with the kids.

In addition to physical and mental work there is *spiritual* preparation, however, and what we do not do any more is prepare spiritually.

The word "spiritual" scares some people and raises unreal expectations for others. This is not a New Age book; it is a Jewish one. It suggests that you follow no regimen beyond the normal ones that Jewish travelers have traditionally included in their journeys to Israel. They are updated, of course, but they are perfectly consistent with mainstream Jewish practice. Despite the word "spiritual," they are perfectly rational as well, and exactly what you would recommend to your best friends.

There are different kinds of journeys. We go on business trips or we go away "for pleasure." We have obligatory family outings as well as weekend jaunts and day trips to the country. Newspapers herald presidential campaign swings and denounce senatorial junkets to fancy places at taxpayers' expense. Our vocabulary is filled with descriptive terms that set off one kind of trip from another.

The trip you are about to make is properly called a pilgrimage. As outmoded as it sounds, you are about to be a pilgrim to a holy site.

READING TWO

The World Doesn't Really Look Like That

What does the world look like? Many years ago, I asked my kids that question, and couldn't believe their answer. "The world," they said, "is a tiny ball in space, with clouds that swirl around it. It gets smaller or larger depending on the speed and direction of the space vehicle taking its picture."

That is not the image I received in high school. For me, the world was a double-page map in an atlas, that I later learned was called the Mercator projection. You remember it: a two-dimensional replica of the earth's surface with a crease down the middle that wipes out the eastern fifth of the Atlantic. When you open the atlas, your eye naturally falls on Western Europe, the focus of the right-hand page. My high school classroom sported a globe as well, but no one ever consulted it. We didn't seriously believe that the world looked that way. For the purposes of tests—which was all that mattered—we were expected to memorize the spaces on the atlas version. The world appeared flattened out and elongated at the edges, as if someone had taken a rolling pin to the earth and stretched it into a piece of dough, colored in the countries, scored it vertically and horizontally with lines of latitude and longitude, and baked it solid. It was only a matter of time until someone else took a cookie cutter to the whole thing to make it into a jigsaw puzzle, so kids like me could memorize its shape. No one ever told us that the world doesn't even remotely look like that.

Though it purports to be an objective measure of the world's surface, the Mercator projection was designed as a political instrument for nineteenth-century British colonialism. Mercator was a geographer, but his geography was governed by his nationalism. He made England the center of his map, so that distance away from zero degrees longitude measures distance from the very heart of the British Empire.

Think about it. When you fly across the Atlantic, you do not feel noticeable jolts every time you cross the lines of longitude. The lines are not really there—they are just convenient ways to chart where things are. Lines of latitude are inherently logical, since the equator is the center of the earth relative to the axis around which the earth spins. Distance from the equator really does measure something real: the relationship of a place to the sun, and therefore the relative degree of heat. But distance from zero degrees longitude is arbitrary. There is no center to the earth's surface on the east-west axis—unless, of course, you live in Greenwich.

The Mercator map of the world was colored back

then, mostly with red. Red was used for British colonies, so that glancing at the map was enough to convince you of the far-flung nature of England's holdings. Pity the poor Asians, whose continent was marginal bits of colonial territory at the two edges of the world, not the most populated land mass on earth with such proud and ancient cultures as those of India, Japan, China, and Indonesia.

As someone at *The New Yorker* magazine figured out one day, the world doesn't have to look like that. In what would perhaps be the most famous cartoon ever made, it published an edition with a Saul Steinberg drawing showing what the world looks like according to the map New Yorkers carry around in their own parochial heads: Lots of detail and space for everything east of the Hudson, a little bit of New Jersey across the river, and then some wheat fields, mountains, cacti and palm trees spread out here and there—marking the Plains, the Rockies, and the entire southwest United States.

The New Yorker was poking fun at its readership but it illustrated the all-important difference between maps and territory. The actual terrain where we live or travel is our *territory*; *maps* are arbitrary ways we picture it. And, as we shall see, we need more than one picture.

READING THREE
Choosing the Right Map

Mapmaking is a tricky business, and not always a light-hearted one. In 1967, for instance, after Israel took possession of the West Bank and the Golan Heights, Israeli cartographers redrew maps of Greater Israel, in which the West Bank Arab town of Nablus reappeared as biblical Shechem, the age-old capital of what Prime Minister Begin began calling the territories of Judea and Samaria. *The New York Times* continued to call it Nablus and referred to the territories as "occupied."

A less serious, but equally enlightening instance occurs when people are asked to draw a map of their neighborhood. People who live far from the office take an early train to work and spend little time at home. They draw a simple map with boxes representing their homes and the railroad station, and a criss-cross line standing for the train track that carries them back and forth from their office in the city. To judge by their map, they live in a wasteland miles away from everything else.

COMMUTERS' MAP

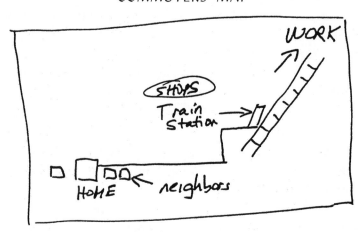

Parents who stay home to take care of their children, however, spend large parts of the day in the car driving car pools and keeping the household going. They tend to draw crowded maps with schools, stores, doctors' offices, and friends' houses.

HOUSEHOLDERS' MAP

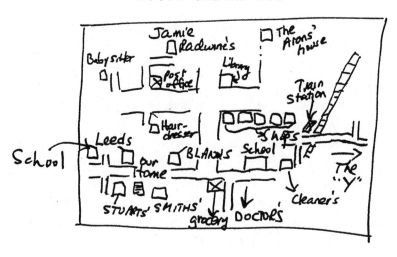

Children have their own selective perception. Their world is made of relatively empty space with hardly any connective roads joining points of interest. After all, they don't have to figure out how to get anywhere. They just climb into the back seat and climb back out again when new destinations magically appear outside their window. And their destinations are few: home, school, friend's house and candy store!

CHILDREN'S MAP

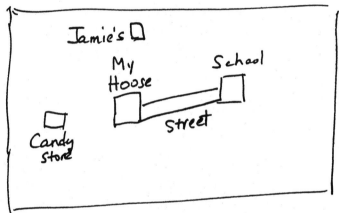

Which map, then, is the right one? The answer is: they all are. New families moving into the suburbs would do well to collect all three maps and allocate them to appropriate family members as they learn their way around town. Commuters find the householders' map confusing. Householders find the commuters' maps inadequate. Maps are properly chosen when they help us accomplish what we want to do. They need not accurately describe the features of the landscapes that exist independently of our needs.

READING FOUR

A Jewish Map for Jewish Pilgrims

Since maps help us do things, we carry more than one of them inside our heads, and choose the one that will most likely help us do what we have to do. When you open the morning newspapers, you glance at the *weather map* to see what the coming weekend will offer in the way of sunshine. For a brief moment, the world is reduced to a series of weather fronts, its highs and lows enclosed by black lines called isobars that dip down like inverted bell curves into the country's mid-section, and move like sound waves from west to east.

Go on a trip, however, and you buy *road maps* that define the countryside in black and red stripes called highways. *Relief maps* ignore the highways but provide elevation peaks, often in three dimensions so you can actually see how high the mountains are. *Elevation maps* rate hikers' routes as easy, moderate or difficult, and *bicyclers' maps* combine elevation and highway systems to measure how arduous a journey will be.

We are all mapmakers. We all carry around inside our heads a virtual atlas filled with imaginary pages that we consult with regularity as we make our way through the spaces of our lives.

One of the spaces of a Jewish life is *Eretz Yisrael*, the land of Israel. I think I've always known that the Mercator projection was not really *my* map. I am inexorably drawn to the contours of the Jewish map of being, where all roads lead to Jerusalem. I have been praying for Jerusalem all my life. To this day I cry when I hear *Y'rushalayim Shel Zahav* ("Jerusalem of Gold"), the most beautiful song in the world, I sometimes think, composed to celebrate the centrality of Jerusalem. Up north in Israel is the Sea of Galilee, the *Kinneret*, the sea around whose shores my ancestors built the earliest synagogues. It is watered by the Jordan, now a tiny rivulet, but once the mighty waterway where Na'aman the leper bathed under Elisha's watchful eye. Isaiah walked the streets of Tel Aviv, for all I know (even though there was no Tel Aviv yet) and for sure, Elijah's ghost still haunts the caves of Mount Carmel where he once challenged the false prophets of Ba'al. Today, Eged buses roar around the bend as they enter Haifa's harbor. Every time I pass it, I half expect a wizened face with a windswept visage and an arm holding a staff to stop the bus in its tracks: Elijah the prophet, come again.

To the left of where Elijah would be standing, on the Mediterranean side of the highway, your eye encounters the remnant of more modern history: the rusty hulk of an immigrant ship, from which *Ma'pilim*, the émigrés who had fled Hitler's inferno, poured ashore illegally past British blockades.

This is just Jerusalem, the *Galil* (the Galilee), and the Haifa area. I haven't even mentioned the Negev where Abraham and Sarah traveled back and forth in search of water, and which David Ben-Gurion called home; or the mystic alleyways of Safed, where Isaac Luria ushered in Shabbat to the gorgeous poetry his friend had written, a song we sing in synagogue services world over, even now: *L'kha Dodi*.

Forget the Mercator projection. What do I know—or care—about Greenwich, England or lines of longitude or red-blotched colonies? The neural pathways of my brain are engraved with a Jewish map: the map of my life's destiny.

READING FIVE

The Jewish Map of Jewish Space and Time

I said before that maps are just arbitrary lines joining together dots of one kind or another. What gives a map its character is the feature that is common to all the points. Suppose an infant takes a crayon and scribbles it randomly through the space on a blank piece of paper. You do not get a map. Maps occur when someone intentionally joins together certain points, and *only* certain points, all of which measure something specific: the places where the land meets the sea (you get a map of the coastline) or the sites where many people dwell (you get a map of cities, joined together by highways).

The question for every map is twofold: what *kind* of locations are being joined? And why?

The Jewish map connects places that figure prominently in what we call our sacred history. Some of them are points in the Diaspora: Sura and Pumbedita, the schools just outside Baghdad where rabbis lived and worked in ancient Babylonia; or Auschwitz, the site of evil where so many of our people perished just because they were Jews. Visitors to Spain can relive the Spanish golden age in the old Jewish quarter of Cordova. Prague still houses the sixteenth-century *Altneuschul*, a medieval synagogue that looks like a fortress and boasts a famous external clock where the hands run "backwards" following hour markings in Hebrew letters that obey the rules of Hebrew script and read from left to right, "counterclockwise."

But most of our sacred sites lie inside the territory we now call Israel. Jews have imagined it for centuries, journeying there when they could, picturing it when they couldn't visit.

Once upon a time, and not so long ago, the pictures of Israel were fabrications made up of hints found in sacred scripture. What, after all, could Rashi, our eleventh-century commentator, know of the real shape of *Eretz Yisrael*? He lived before Marco Polo ushered in the age of exploration. Near the end of his life, the Crusaders traveled back and forth from Paris to Jerusalem, but prior to that, Rashi had few people to ask about the land. Still, he yearned to know what it looked like. When he wrote his commentary to the Torah, he drew this map of the land based on what he found in the book of Numbers.

RASHI'S MAP

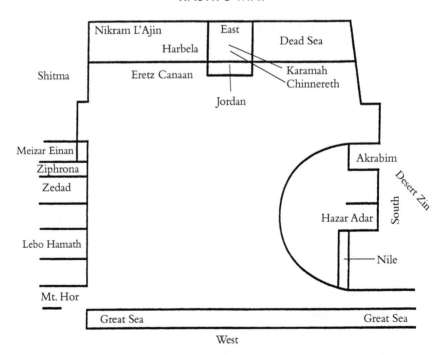

Source: Hebrew Maps of the Holy Land *by E. & G. Weintraub, Brüder Hollinek, Wein, 1992.*

On this map, Rashi was thinking in geometric patterns with biblical sites (including the Mediterranean—"The Great Sea") slotted in like boxes. The second-century geographer Ptolemy had already developed the convention by which maps were drawn with north at the top of the page. But by Rashi's time, east went at the top, to indicate the centrality of Jerusalem, city of the East. Since the text says that Israel extends all the way to Egypt, the borders on Rashi's map are the Jordan River on the east; the "Great Sea" on the west; some relatively obscure cities up north; and the Nile, together with the desert, in the south.

In Spain, around the same time, Judah Halevi was writing what became perhaps the most famous poem of a Jew's yearning to revisit the sacred space of our homeland. "My heart is in the East," it began, "but I am in the uttermost West." Legend later recalled that he eventually moved there, only to be trampled to death by a passing Arab horseman as he bent over to kiss the land to which he had been so intensely attached all his life. A thousand years of Jewish readers would memorize the opening stanza of his poem, composed some time before he left Spain: "I am in the west, but my heart is in the east."

READING SIX
Becoming a Jewish Pilgrim

We Jews still consult the pages of our Jewish atlas, the one our people filled with sacred sites. It is the map we use if we are pilgrims, and if you are reading this book, that is precisely what you are, whether you yet know it or not.

The word "pilgrim" has fallen on hard times. It entered our modern vocabulary through such famous works as Geoffrey Chaucer's *The Canterbury Tales* or John Bunyan's *Pilgrim's Progress*. From Chaucer, we inherited the medieval model of going far from home to get directly in touch with sacred space. Bunyan gave us the pilgrimage of life, a journey from birth to death, with God as our final destination. What the two have in common is the idealized notion of heading for some ultimate, distant, and destined place that is the whole point of being here. America's settlers called themselves "pilgrims" because they thought they were coming to the promised land.

These are not Jewish examples, but change the cast of characters a little, and Jews might easily have composed similar accounts. Western Christian literature depicts pilgrims en route to cures at Lourdes, but Chasidic Jews made similar journeys to their rebbes. When Crusaders conquered Jerusalem in 1099, Christian pilgrims began once again to flock to the land where Jesus had lived and died. But Jews had been making pilgrimage there for 2,000 years. Ever since biblical days, the holidays of Pesach, Sukkot and Shavuot had been expressly designated *r'galim*, from the Hebrew word *regel*, foot, because they were the occasions to travel to Jerusalem and "set foot" there.

As for our lives as sacred journeys, it was Abraham who was first summoned to leave his father's home and "go to the land that I [God] will show you." Both Jacob and Joseph died outside the land of Israel, but they made their heirs promise to bring their bones home for reinterment on sacred soil. We have seen the eleventh-century poet Judah Halevi bemoan the fact that he lived in "the uttermost West" far away from the east where his heart was. But by the twelfth-century, the Crusader routes that brought Christians to Jerusalem opened up Holy Land travel for Jews too. The most famous pilgrim of all, Benjamin of Tudela (twelfth century), traveled for somewhere between five and fourteen years, leaving us a detailed account of Jewish life not only in Israel, but everywhere he went, as far away as present-day Iran.

Pilgrimage is therefore Jewish to the core. Muslims make a *hajj* to Mecca; Christians walk the Via Dolorosa; Hindus bathe in the Ganges; but Jews make pilgrimages also. We have been doing it ever since biblical times.

Some years ago, a sign in New York's Lower East Side announced an organization called the "*Ma'alin B'kodesh Society*." Its business was transporting the remains of Jews who die in the Diaspora to burial sites in Israel. Even if they made no pilgrimages while alive, they might at least make one after death. *Ma'alin b'kodesh* is the beginning of a talmudic aphorism meaning, "You may add to holiness; you may not decrease it," but the society was using it to mean "going up to holiness." In Jewish geography, moving to Israel is called *aliyah* because *aliyah* means ascending: ascending to greater holiness.

SET 2

READING SEVEN
Pilgrim or Tourist?

If life is a pilgrimage, it is also a story with ourselves as the central characters. Teenagers who visit Israel and tell their tale many years after are likely to relate that Israel made them who they were. Those of us who are middle-aged or older go with the sense that the chapters of our lives are being written faster and faster, and that we need to reserve a place for Israel before the plot gets completely written. True, the *Ma'alin B'kodesh Society* will move you to Israel after you die. But even Jews who are marginally religious are likely to wake up one day and know, somehow, that it matters very much that they go to Israel while they are still alive. Their story would be incomplete without it. No wonder tourism is Israel's largest industry.

But tourism is the wrong word for what Jews do when they go to Israel. These are not diversions, these UJA missions, youth-group summers, congregational trips, and bar or bat mitzvah journeys. They are life decisions. Thinking of yourself as a tourist at such a moment wholly misses the point.

For tourism is the ultimate exercise in nothingness. We leave as tourists to "get away from it all." We "do nothing," even "vegetate," or "recharge our batteries," for a successful return to work. Tourists are despised for their garish manners and bloated self-importance. They are dolts armed with cameras, ravaging the very land they visit, trashing it with litter. Tourists are lured by the devious voice of commercial enterprise, which will say anything to attract its trade.

They are not pulled by the still small voice of conscience that sends them to Israel because it is time to head home. "For thousands of years," said the old El Al Airlines commercial, "Jews have celebrated Passover with the promise 'Next year in Jerusalem!' Make it *this* year in Jerusalem. Prices have never been lower." Thus Madison Avenue converts the hope for the end of time into a whim for vacation time.

Tourists go to Jerusalem the way they go to Disneyworld: not to pray at its sacred Western Wall, but to take pictures of other people praying there. They will rearrange the scenery, and even the people, so as to bring back the best picture. I remember vividly one Tisha B'av in Jerusalem. It was dark, but the thousands of flash attachments exploding their light at the old men wailing on the ground lit up the Wall like the Fourth of July. I tried in vain to explain to my children that second only to Yom Kippur, this was the most important fast in all of Judaism; that this is a time of national grief for the destruction of both of our Temples, and the day on which Jews are said to have been expelled from Spain. It looked instead like a movie set or a safari, with hoards of Americans carrying camcorders to catch all the action.

I know, not all tourists are that bad; and not all pilgrims are any better. I am idealizing things somewhat, pushing the two types to their extreme. Thoughtless pilgrims can litter the ground with lunch debris, and honest tourists can respect the lives of the people they visit. But on a spectrum, visitors to a place tend toward one or the other extreme. If they come for enjoyment, a break from the routine before returning home to work, they are tourists—perhaps harmless, perhaps not. Pilgrims come because being in this place is part of who they are, a necessary segment in the story of their lives. If they are on a journey, not to *leave* home, but to *come* home to a deeper place in their soul, then they are pilgrims.

Most Jews visit Israel as pilgrims, not as tourists. At some point, it dawns on them that they are returning home—home to their history, home to their people, home to the place where it all began.

READING EIGHT

Sights and Sites

For tourists, the world is made of "sights"; for pilgrims, it consists of "sites." A "sight" exists only to be seen, whereas a "site" retains its existence even if no one ever sees it. Some things are both, the massive Sinai desert, for example. It is monumental in scope (a sight); but something majestic happened to our people on one of its mountains (making it very much a site).

Sights have universal appeal. You arrive at a sight and cannot take your eyes off it. It is visibly magnificent—the Pacific Redwoods, say, or the Grand Canyon, or even an oddity in nature or in art. It may even be a beautiful surprise—what we call, appropriately enough, "a sight for sore eyes." "What's that funny looking building?" visitors to New York ask about the Flatiron Building, a triangular structure so thin at one end it looks like a stiff wind would blow it over. It is a sight. All you need to appreciate a sight are the eyes with which to see it.

Sites, however, can be so ordinary in appearance as to escape detection. They look pretty much like everything round about them. You have to know about them in advance, usually because you have some connection to them, as when an American asks, "Where is the site of the Battle of Bunker Hill?" Authorities put up "On this site . . ." markers so that visitors can find what they are looking for. We arrive at them committed to their importance, and may, in retrospect, be disappointed at how commonplace they look. We may even go home complaining, "It was so ordinary!"

For Native Americans, the redwoods exemplify a place that is both a sight (the trees are awesome) and a site (the spirits live there; it is home). Some years ago, the federal government licensed the logging industry to drive its daily take of timber through a forest that Native Americans held sacred. The government claimed that the landscape looked exactly like the other areas round about; what difference, then, would a simple road make? But they missed the point, by treating it like a sight. For American Indians, it was a site, the place out of which the tribes had originally sprung, and home now to their ancestors. The government's road was like a two-lane highway through the house where your mother and father had raised you.

Israel is filled with sights. At every turn is something worthy of a perfect picture. It is, after all, a gorgeous land with impeccably blue sky, rocky hills that lead off splendidly into a desert expanse to the south and snowcapped mountains in the north. The wilderness where the Israelites wandered remains as hostile now as it was then. You will know this full well by stopping at the aptly named Dead Sea, the lowest point on earth, where Sodom, the arch-evil city of sin, once stood. But even there, you will find magnificent oases like Ein Gedi, and far away, as the desert ends in the south, the clearest water in the world greets snorkeling visitors at Eilat. If you want sights, Israel will satisfy. But Jews who are pilgrims go for *sites*. We go because what happened there is part of what makes us who we are.

Tourists capture sights in living color. Pilgrims are themselves captured by the site's holiness. They are unexpectedly carried away by what is simultaneously the story of the site and the story of themselves.

We may begin as tourists or even as wary pilgrims in the making, hesitant to trash our Western-style sense of being in control. We may go only marginally invested in the story we are about to experience—certainly not expecting to kiss the Wall, actually pray at someone's tomb, or dip our hands into the soil where Isaac dug his wells and modern day *chalutzim* (pioneers) made the desert bloom. But we may be surprised. The land of Israel may have its own way upon us. We learn to see its sites, not just its sights, to appreciate its enduring sacred character, to know it for what it is: the land toward which we have been heading all our lives.

READING NINE

Having a Home

The desire to return home runs deep in the human spirit. John Denver sold a million records singing, "Country road, take me home, to the place I belong." Home is where the heart is; it is the place they have to let you in; it is the single spot on earth where you can stop running because you are "home free."

And "homing" is human to its core, because most life forms have no permanent home at all. Flowers grow wild; they naturally spread out to protect against being uprooted from a single place and perishing forever. Colorado Aspen trees send root systems underground for miles; common garden mint will take over your own yard and the neighbor's too; Ivy League colleges get their name from a ground cover than attaches to walls and climbs tall buildings to overrun new terrain. Animals at least build makeshift homes, but mostly for their young, or sometimes to establish colonies like beehives and anthills, where strength lies in numbers. But they rarely last beyond the season. When animals more or less return in spring, we grow attached to them precisely because we think they are being human. They become pets when we domesticate them, by making them part of our domiciles, our homes.

Our earliest, but still prehuman, ancestors were no different, but as they grew to be distinctly human they developed real homes. Homes carry memories. We get attached to them. "Homeward bound," Simon and Garfunkel sang. "Home, where my thought's escapin', home where the music's playin', home where my love lies waitin' silently for me." As an earlier ballad had it, "Be it ever so humble, there's no place like home."

The book of Genesis is about a lot of things, but mostly, it is a tale of human beginnings. It therefore strikes an early note on this distinctively human theme of having a home. Of all the creatures God makes, only Adam and Eve receive a home: Eden, the idyllic home we all wish we had. Human tragedy occurs when they are driven from it. The tragedy of homelessness follows regularly thereafter. When Cain kills Abel, he is sentenced to wander the earth: an eternal hunter, not the uniquely human hero of the Bible who settles into landedness. Noah was set adrift, with the entire earth potentially dissolved in endless rain. Thank God for the dove, a divine harbinger of news that land was still left, somewhere, on which, at last, to settle again.

Abraham's father, Terach, has a home, but Abraham is not at home in it. Joseph is sold into bondage to a land not his own, and when he dies, he insists that his brothers at least bury his bones back home when they return. In the meantime, they will suffer the ultimate curse, becoming strangers in a strange land. Only with the Exodus will Jacob's children finally launch their journey home, in a tale that will take the rest of Torah to unfold.

The whole of the Bible, not just the Torah, can fairly be described as a logbook on how we Jews found a home, then lost it in exile, and then returned. Our most famous hero, Moses, is quintessentially in search of a home he never reaches. Like Abraham in his father's house, Moses knows he doesn't belong in the home of his adoptive father, Pharaoh. He escapes to the desert, then is summoned to bring God's people home. He dies looking out across the Jordan at the home he seeks but will never inhabit.

Everything else in the biblical narrative is an extended footnote to this theme of home. Joshua conquers it, the Judges secure it, David and Solomon solidify it, the rest of the kings lose it, Ezra and Nehemiah recover it. The prophets justify its loss and predict (and then celebrate) its return. Deuteronomy sums up all of Jewish history with this single simple paradigm:

> My father was a wandering Aramean. He went down into Egypt to sojourn there. . . . There he became a nation, great, mighty, and numerous. The Egyptians persecuted us . . . and we cried out to God, who listened to us . . . and delivered us. God brought us . . . to the land flowing with milk and honey.

Look at the contrasts! We began as wanderers, but ended as a landed people. Two thousand years of Jewish readers learned that God's greatest gift was a place called home, and in our time, we have returned there.

READING TEN

Returning Home

The curse of homelessness has haunted our People long enough that every schoolchild knows the term, "wandering Jew." The Rabbis encoded this idea early in Jewish thought under the technical designation *galut*, meaning "exile." Since then, we have noisily and stubbornly defined being human as the condition of seeking to be at home, not in exile. Our greatest contribution to the moral standards of humanity is not our discovery of monotheism, but the insistent charge to remember when we had no home. "We were slaves in the land of Egypt," and therefore we insist on a Jewish mandate to end slavery and homelessness for everyone.

Our obsession with home has not necessarily led all of us to settle in our homeland. Even the Rabbis of the Talmud, the very sages who speak unstintingly of exile, lived mostly in Babylonia (modern-day Iraq), and their successors lived in Spain, Italy, Germany, France, or any other land where they were welcomed. Many Jews really did go to live in Israel, of course, but even for those who did not, Israel became a real-life example of where you always knew you belonged. If they didn't move there, they visited; if they couldn't visit, they prayed for it, dreamed of it, and held it softly in their thoughts from far away. For them all, however, Israel was "home."

Not all religions celebrate home-centered geography. Christianity, for instance, successfully became the official religion of the Roman Empire, but at a price: As a global religion, it lost the simplicity of its Jewish home-based origins. Jesus, the Jew, met with his disciples in private homes, and prayed with them as they ate together. Early Christian churches too were homes, not lavish buildings. With the imperialization of Christianity, however, churches became vast imperial chambers and Christian liturgy evolved into pageantry-filled spectacles. Judaism, however, retained its earliest ideal in which homes were so sacred that they had been likened to the Temple.

Every holiday was outfitted with its "home" side: the Passover seder, Shabbat Kiddush, the backyard sukkah, Chanukah candles, Havdalah, apples and honey on Rosh Ha-shanah. The synagogue too was outfitted to be a "home" of sorts: a place where wayfarers might spend the night, and where, therefore, home ceremonials like Shabbat Kiddush and candle-lighting became the norm. In Hebrew, the three most common designations for a synagogue are *beit hamidrash*, *beit hat'fillah*, and *beit hak'nesset*, not just a *place* for "study," "prayer" and "gathering," but a *home* (a *bayit*) for these three vital functions.

And when we die, we go again to a home, an eternal one, as Judaism imagines it, ideally, buried in Israel itself.

The master metaphor of "home" is a Jewish gift to the world. Life is the process of heading home to God. Along the way, we have a taste of being with God—the experience of earthly homes where we know we are welcome, where no one hunts us down, where we welcome others the way Abraham did the strangers who arrived at his tent in the heat of the noonday sun.

And to keep all this in the forefront of our consciousness, we visit Israel on occasion: as pilgrims, really going home.

READING ELEVEN

A Pilgrim's Geography: Out of the Wilderness

Geography matters. It shapes our thinking. In North America, for instance, life on the frontier makes the West wild. Life on the plains brings wind storms, tornadoes, and vastness beyond measure. New York City means concrete and crowding, while "laid-back" Southern California enjoys perpetual sunshine.

But geography is partly what we make it. Jews in *Eretz Yisrael* have been seized by the shape of the land, but the land became what they wanted it to be, through the force of their imagination. Jews in Israel are like Americans in Montana, the Big Sky State. The sky looks bigger there, partly because people who move there imagine it to be so, and therefore, they see it that way. So too, Jerusalem's holiness is partly innate, and partly designed by people who want to make it as sacred as they think it already is.

Most people start their pilgrimage to Israel in Jerusalem these days. They get off the plane at Ben-Gurion Airport and move immediately by car to our sacred center, *Ir Hakodesh* (as we call it), "The Holy City." But that is not how Jews of previous generations arrived there. Before plane travel, they approached it over land or by sea, making Jerusalem the end of the journey not the beginning.

We lose something by starting out where we really ought to end up. Jewish law prohibits shortcuts through sacred places: shortcuts can shortchange us.

Once upon a time, pilgrims got to Jerusalem only after trekking through the wilderness first, not at all unlike the Israelites who journeyed from Egypt.

MAP OF SOUTHERN ISRAEL

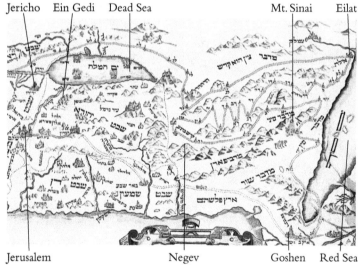

Jericho   Ein Gedi   Dead Sea   Mt. Sinai   Eilat

Jerusalem   Negev   Goshen   Red Sea

South of Jerusalem is the Negev, the Judean desert. Imagine heading endlessly north, and only after many weeks, without watches, calendars, or anyone who had ever gone before you, seeing the capital from the distance. The Negev ends just barely south of the Old City, and is the northernmost extension of the vast Sinai peninsula, where the Israelite ex-slaves first met God. In many ways, 3,000 years haven't changed the terrain very much. You still pass

Bedouin who look like modern-day versions of Abraham, Isaac or Jacob. The sand still swirls in the wind, and heat storms still blow northward into Jerusalem homes. Standing on the limitless desert sand, you can still see an infinity of stars, both of which—sand and stars—God showed Abraham as a sign of how numerous his progeny would some day be.

Just south of Jerusalem, as the road through the Negev starts to climb upward, you still see the caves where the Dead Sea sects lived after leaving Jerusalem because they thought it corrupt—just like New York or Los Angeles in the eyes of some parts of Middle America. You pass the Dead Sea, "the lowest place on earth," says the sign. You will also pass Ein Gedi, where David and his army once hid in cool caves—an oasis, really, where his ancestors watered their flock and dug their wells.

MAP OF NORTHERN ISRAEL

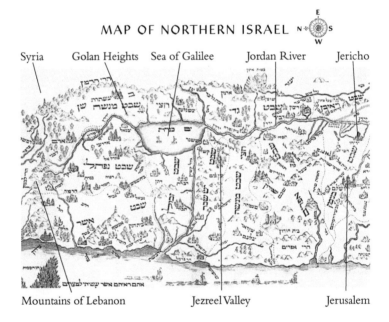

Syria   Golan Heights   Sea of Galilee   Jordan River   Jericho

Mountains of Lebanon   Jezreel Valley   Jerusalem

Other pilgrims, later in time, came from the North, not the South. Before the Babylonian exile (587 B.C.E.), residents north of Jerusalem constituted a separate state that did not recognize Jerusalem as its capital, so they made no pilgrimage to Jerusalem. But some fifty years later, exile ended, and waves of Jews slowly came home. Jerusalem was now the capital for a unified country, and it attracted streams of pilgrim-farmers from up north. After the invasion of Alexander the Great (334 B.C.E.), Israel entered the cultural orbit of

Greece, with ties to Greek-speaking Jews in Asia Minor, the area north of Israel. From there, members of a flourishing Jewish Diaspora would have headed south over the mountains in present-day Lebanon or Syria, and then down the Golan Heights into the Jordan Valley. Following the Jordan south, they too would have come to the city that captured their dreams.

MAP OF EASTERN ISRAEL

Jordan River   Jordanian Plain   Jericho

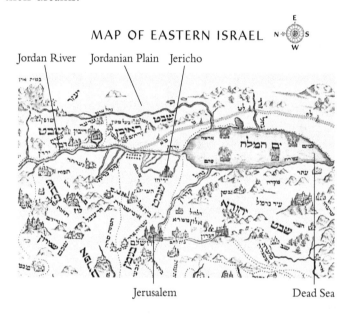

Jerusalem   Dead Sea

Jews once came from farther east too. The first-century Jewish historian Josephus reports an unexplained arrival of a band of archers on horseback, who announced, to his surprise, that they were Jews from Babylonia. Whoever these Jews were, they hardly looked Jewish to Josephus. They had followed trade routes from the Tigris-Euphrates valley, through present-day Jordan, and then across the Jordan River into Jerusalem.

From the perspective of Jerusalemites, the Judean desert to the south, the Syrian mountains to the north, and Jordanian plain to the east were all just different degrees of wilderness. Jerusalem was still tiny compared to the great cities where many of these pilgrims had begun their journey, but it was already the Jewish center of gravity, and it has grown, both in grandeur and in significance, ever since.

READING TWELVE

A Pilgrim's Geography:
From the Coastland to the Galil

Another approach to Jerusalem transported pilgrims east-ward from a seaport along the Mediterranean coast. Those of us who fly briefly over it after traveling all night across the Atlantic find it hard to imagine what the "Great Sea" (as the Mediterranean was known) meant to Jews in ancient times. The classical cultures of Greece and Rome grew up along its shores; to a Greek, Morocco was the other end of the world, and the distance from Algiers to Rome was like Moscow to Washington, a far-off capital of a rival empire that shared the world's destiny. As late as the ninth century, Muslims tried to squeeze the life out of Christian Europe by controlling the Great Sea's waters. (One Muslim geographer boasted, "The Christians cannot float a plank on it!") It was the life-blood of ancient times.

MAP OF WESTERN ISRAEL

Sea of Galilee Caesaria Jaffa Jerusalem Ashkelon Philistines

Mt. Carmel, Haifa

Since there were limits to how much land a pilgrim would willingly traverse, Jews from Italy and North Africa preferred to travel on ships that would dock in Israel's harbors.

These ports were mostly ancient, going back to the Philistines who arrived by ship from Greece about 1200 B.C.E., and included in their midst legendary biblical enemies like Goliath of Gath. With the arrival of Phoenicians up north around Lebanon, and then Greeks and Romans all along the coast, old harbors were enlarged, and new ones sprang up.

The word "Palestine" comes from "Philistine," so perhaps it is appropriate that the Gaza strip, once the stronghold of Philistine culture, is now Palestinian through and through. As you head north from Gaza, however, you reach ancient harbors that are thoroughly Israeli: Jaffa, Caesaria, and Haifa. Jaffa stretches back thirty-six centuries, Haifa thirty-four, Caesaria (only!) twenty-four. Classical empires depended on natural ports to ply their trade, including a regular human cargo of Jewish pilgrims coming from Africa or Europe to holy Israel soil.

The Rabbis were in awe of the Mediterranean. They knew it intimately, partly because they too ran businesses that depended on shipping. Furthermore, after the Romans defeated the Jews and destroyed the Temple in 70 C.E., rabbinic culture was relocated to Yavneh, now a suburb of Tel Aviv, and not far from the port of Jaffa. The sun sets over the Mediterranean by virtually melting into its blue-green water. Our spiritual legacy from those Rabbis still contains a blessing to be said when the Great Sea comes into view.

Over the centuries, one army after another landed its troops on the Mediterranean coast and then proceeded to conquer the land—only to be conquered in turn, as stronger armies arrived later. The Romans took their turn landing here to put down the Jewish rebellion in 70 C.E., and then again, with heavy reinforcements, to fight the Bar Kokhba revolt sixty-five years later. This time, the troops stayed, and a provincial government was set up in the lush farming territory around the *Kinneret,* the Sea of Galilee. The Rabbis followed the government inland, abandoning Yavneh for the area around Tiberias, the main city on the western slope of the sea.

Jews call the Galilee "the Galil." It comprises almost the entire northern part of Israel from the Mediterranean coast, on the east, to the Jordan, on the west. It abuts Leb-

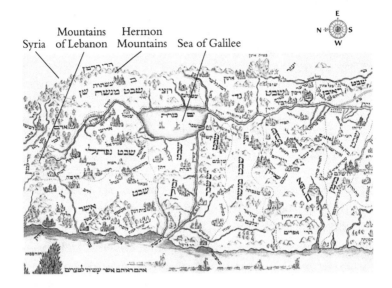

anon in the northwest, and Syria in the northeast. It is dominated by the Sea of Galilee. East of the Jordan is the Transjordan, now the Kingdom of Jordan and not Israel at all, though some of the twelve tribes are said to have lived there in biblical days. If you take the Jordan south, the Kingdom of Jordan continues on your left, while on your right, you see the West Bank. If you take the Jordan north, you pass through the *Kinneret*. Farther up still, you eventually reach its head waters in the mountains of Syria, passing through the Golan Heights.

Jews had settled the entire Galilee during the conquest of Canaan, then fought for the land under Judges like Deborah who prevailed over the Canaanites in the Jezreel Valley, under the shadow of Mt. Tabor. Later still, the prophet Elisha had Na'aman, a Syrian general, bathe in the Jordan in order to be cured of disease. With the Roman relocation, Jews flocked here again to be near the administrative center of the country.

Watered by the Jordan, which carried torrents of melted snow from mountains up north, the area became Israel's breadbasket. Pilgrims from its cities reached Jerusalem with relative ease. To this day, the Galil houses most of Israel's ancient synagogue ruins, a testimonial to its status as the place where so many people made their home. When medieval mystics arrived as émigrés after their expulsion from Spain, they settled in Safed, a mountain community west of the *Kinneret* (but still in the Galil) adding yet a new cultural flavor to the centuries-old mix that northern Israel became.

In time, the once prosperous breadbasket became malaria-infested swampland, which twentieth-century immigrants drained to build *kibbutzim*. On the south shore of the *Kinneret*, you can still visit Deganya, the grand-daddy of the *Kibbutz* Movement, started by laborers who were also poets and spiritual visionaries.

As modern-day pilgrims, you will probably spend more time in and around the *Kinneret* than you will in any other area, save Jerusalem itself, the final stop on any pilgrim's itinerary.

SET 3

READING THIRTEEN
Jerusalem: The Center of the World

Some 3,000 years ago, Jerusalem was a mountain city of the Jebusites, one of the tribes whom the Israelites encountered when they settled the land. About 1000 B.C.E., King David made it his capital. His son Solomon built the Temple on one of its larger hilly areas, Mt. Zion, whence the name Zion (and later still, Zionist) is derived.

As our holiest city (and holy too to Christianity and Islam), there are more legends about Jerusalem than about any other city in Western history, maybe in the world. The midrash hints at its mythic richness when it says that Jerusalem has seventy names, including *Shalom*, "Peace"; *Marom*, "Heights"; *M'nuchah*, "Rest"; *Yafeh*, "Beautiful"; *Y'didut*, "Beloved"; *M'tsudah*, "Fortress"; *Gilah*, "Joy"; *Gan Adonai*, "Garden of God"; *Ir Hayonah*, "City of Doves"; *Kiryah Ne'emanah*, "Faithful City"; *Ir Hatzedek*, "City of Righteousness"; *Gei Chizayon*, "Valley of Vision," *Daltot Ha'amim*, "Doorway for the World's Peoples"; and even *Eden*, the garden of gardens itself.

Today's Jerusalem features flowers everywhere; gardeners

King David builds Jerusalem · · · · · **King Josiah/Deuteronomy** · · · · **Babylonian Exile** · · · · · **Ezekiel in Babylonia** · · · ·

C. 1000 B.C.E.

621 B.C.E.

587 B.C.E.

learned to water them one by one when this was still the upward region of the Judean desert, and Jerusalemites never kept the tap running because water was so scarce.

In its relationship to our people, Jerusalem is most frequently likened to a mother. She is sometimes thought of also as a young unmarried woman, *b'tulah*, or a bride, *kallah*, and even a barren woman, *akarah*, bereft of her children who languish in exile. She mourns their absence while patiently awaiting their return.

Though David had settled Jerusalem by the tenth century, it took three centuries more for it to emerge as Israel's only sacred center. In 621 B.C.E., King Josiah announced that he had discovered an age-old sacred book (the book of Deuteronomy) demanding that sacrifices be offered only in Jerusalem. Rival shrines in northern sites were successfully rooted out, and from that day onward, no other city has challenged Jerusalem's hegemony in Jewish imagination.

About a century later, the prophet Ezekiel envisioned Jerusalem from his place of exile in Babylonia, calling it, for the first time, God's holy mountain. His idealized geometry placed it literally in the geographic center of the country, leading rabbinic tradition to imagine all of Israel as a set of concentric circles, like ripples of the sacred, emanating outward from the Holy of Holies within the Temple precinct. The Temple disappeared, pummeled into dust by Roman battering rams. The ripples of this destruction continue through time.

The Romans left standing only a single external structure to the west that had been used as a retaining wall for the Temple's foundation. Known as the "Western Wall" and even the "Wailing Wall," Jews now call it simply "the Wall" (in Hebrew, "the *Kotel*"). High above the Wall sits the site where the Temple once stood. It is the most sacred place we know. The axis of the earth is there, the Rabbis said. From there peace will be announced to all the world. No matter how you arrive, it is still the holy mountain, Jerusalem of Gold, the Garden of Eden, and mother to Jews the world over.

READING FOURTEEN

Where You Know that You Feel What You Cannot See

Think of Israel the way pilgrims always have:

- Jerusalem in the center.
- A desert wilderness to the south, where Abraham and Sarah camped, and where Egyptian slaves first made their appearance on their memorable return home.
- A mountain run to the north, still visible from the Galil, and approachable in the foothills called the Golan Heights; it is in the Galil where life went on in farms and mountain towns, from Roman times until our own.
- A coastal plain westward in luscious proximity to the Great Sea. Here lay the commercial hub that connects Israel to civilizations whose ships have docked with ideas and with goods for centuries.
- To the east lay empires that changed hands with every passing century: first Babylonia, then Persia, then Babylonia again, then various Muslim dynasties. It didn't matter. Jews came from one empire or another with equal fervor, crossing the Jordan eventually, passing through Bethlehem perhaps (hence the Christian story of the inn that had no room for Jesus), and then climbing to Jerusalem with the rising sun at their back, so that when they got to the city of their dreams, they saw it sparkling and alive with the brilliant play of golds and yellows.

You will get the history of all these places. Israeli guides are good at that. And you cannot miss the beauty of the landscape. God is good at that! You will not easily miss the pulse of modern life alongside echoes of antiquity in this country that survives history even as it remembers it. What you can so easily miss is a sense of the sacred, without which all of this is just another pretty place with ruins, one more set of things to see before moving on to next year's tourist finds.

Throughout the world, the sacred evokes ritual: bathing in the Ganges; spirit quests in Native American forests; and inserting notes of prayer in the crevices of the *Kotel*. Why not? Should space be any different from time? Whether we notice or not, Shabbat falls every seven days. But because we *want* to notice, we adopt ritual welcomes and farewells as Shabbat comes and goes. Without Kiddush and candles Shabbat steals in too silently to attract attention; without Havdalah, it steals away with equal ease. So too, Yom Kippur or Pesach give us telltale signs of *Kol Nidrei* and seder tunes. Even secular time demands some ritual attention: watching the ball drop on New Year's Eve or blowing out the candles on a birthday cake.

So too with secular space: A visitor to the United States House of Representatives describes being invited by a friendly insider to mount the speaker's podium late one night when no one was in the chamber. "Not a chance," he replied, "It felt like the *bimah* in my synagogue. I couldn't go up there without a blessing, or something." That is exactly how sensitive visitors feel when they walk through the Jaffa Gate into the Old City of Jerusalem or stand on the street where Isaiah walked. "There ought to be a blessing, or something."

There usually is a "blessing, or something." Moses took off his shoes when he saw the burning bush. He might equally well have passed it by with a simple "very interesting," or even whatever word he used for "Wow!" Blessed with cameras, as he was not, we are more likely to settle for a picture. But as we shall see, a picture is not enough. Cameras reproduce the horizon but they cannot show what they cannot see. This book encourages you to get in touch with the dimensions of experience that cannot be seen.

READING FIFTEEN

What I Learned from My Grandfather's Watch

My grandfather taught me to tell time. He worked his whole life for almost nothing. Yet each night he managed to bring home his prized possession: a railroad watch that sparkled in the sun when he let it dangle out of the pocket where it lodged. I used to stare at it from the comfort of his lap.

There was a certain magic about the way he said it worked. Just three hands of different sizes that somehow measured time in hours, minutes, and even seconds.

Years later, I graduated to modern Casio watches that flashed the time more accurately in single digital readouts, and I learned the difference between digital and analog displays. Mercury thermometers, old-time bathroom scales, and railroad watches are analog. They provide a spatial analogy to the flow of time, weight or temperature; as time passes, pounds increase, or temperature rises, an arbitrary marker (hands on a clock, numbers on a scale, and the mercury level in the thermometer) move through a space that is calibrated roughly to correspond to the thing being measured. You can watch time fly, weight change, and temperature alter by keeping your eyes glued to the watch hand, the scale dial, or the thermometer gauge.

But analog indicators are approximate. Computers provide more exact digital readouts. Your watch says 9:42 until, exactly one minute later, it skips to 9:43. The room registers at exactly 87 degrees Fahrenheit. The scale lights up at a precise weight of 107.5 pounds.

Something within us loves precision. We prefer digital measurements even though the world doesn't really work that way. Time does not jolt forward second by second, and both temperature and weight build up slowly. We just like the idea of exactitude. So we pretend that we can arrest changing speed or time or anything else in mid-movement, holding it there until the next precise measurement is reached.

That is the kind of thinking that goes into the formation of religious celebration. We like to know *exactly* when Shabbat begins, a holiday ends, or services commence. Countless brides and grooms have asked their rabbi, "Exactly when in the ceremony do we actually become married?" Secular celebration works the same way. Wanting to know the exact time to ring in the new year, we count down to it, and then erupt with "Happy New Year." Ritual converts the natural flow of time, which is analogic, into the arbitrary, make-believe time of digital precision, by imagining an exact stoppage of time at which an event takes place.

Human celebration, religious or secular, thus requires that we imagine an arbitrary time at which the thing in question is said to occur: the second we really turn twenty-one, the moment of actual sunrise, the time when day magically becomes night. For some time prior, we learn to *anticipate* it—the month of Elul that precedes Rosh Hashanah, the three-week set of Torah readings in synagogue that warn us of Passover's imminent arrival, or the six-week hype before a superbowl. Then just before it arrives, we frenetically increase our attention to the event as we watch it *approach*—getting ready for Rosh Hashanah dinner, cleaning house for the Seder, or preparing the Superbowl party.

And then it arrives: Kiddush with apples and honey, the first page of the Haggadah, or the kick-off for the big game. In all three cases, *anticipation* and then *approach* culminate in ritual *acknowledgment*. We savor the moment only if we have taken requisite care to build up to it, and then to be ready to mark it when it comes.

And if we are successful, we keep the moment alive for a while afterward. With happy events, we speak of an afterglow. But even sad occasions last beyond the moment of ritual closure—a funeral, for instance, provides memories that affect us profoundly for years to come. As much as we have to take care to build up to the moments that matter, we need to nurture the echoes of their occurrence in the recesses of our memories.

READING SIXTEEN

Anticipate, Approach, Acknowledge— and Afterthought

Modern clocks were not invented until the thirteenth or fourteenth century. Until then, people used the equivalent of hourglasses with the flow of water or sand to mark the passing of time. No one ever knew exactly what time it was. Things began when they began and lasted as long as they lasted. Now, by contrast, we are conditioned to move from one thing to another, barely recalling the one we finish, allotting no time to get ready for the one approaching. It's called efficiency.

Matters of the heart and of the spirit, however, cannot be squeezed into a convenient time slot and then quickly put on hold. They require anticipation and approach before they can be acknowledged. They need to be replayed in our memories afterward; otherwise, we rob ourselves of the full depth of these events that mark time's passing. We rob our heirs as well: our children and grandchildren will never know what we have learned if we do not take time to savor it ourselves—and then record it for them.

Traditional ritual compensates for the rush that permeates modern life. It makes us stretch the single moment of the "happening" by preparation and afterthought. It prevents us from exhausting all our energy on a single fleeting moment without attending to the rules and regulations that come before and after. Birthdays, for example, are anticipated by months of sending invitations and planning the party. They are then approached by a day of excitement as last feverish preparations are made (even though the person with the birthday and the family pretend to each other that nothing is going to happen). The birthday highlight (blowing out the candles on the cake) is followed by singing "Happy Birthday," and then cutting and eating the cake—as often as not a poorly made commercial one that no one wants anyway, but which everyone eats anyhow, rather than rudely cutting the ritual short and just going home.

What goes for birthdays, goes for other rituals too. People anticipate New Year's Eve by making dates and reservations in November or December, even to the point of transforming excitement into anxiety. Then they approach the digital moment by watching the ball slowly descend from the tower in Times Square, so that when it does, they can stop the motion magically and enjoy the precise instant when the new year comes into being. But the night is still young. The band keeps playing; the party continues for hours; and there is still New Year's Day, with football games, parties to attend, and a feel of the new year to share with neighbors.

We appreciate the digital moments of ritual only if we pay attention to the preceding build-up of anticipation and approach. Otherwise the moments that matter arrive unheralded. Similarly, those moments matter more if we bask in their glory after they have occurred, and record them before they escape into forgetfulness.

You will appreciate the sacred sites of your pilgrimage if you prepare for them first and let them linger for a while afterward. The magic recipe is therefore, "Anticipate, Approach, Acknowledge, Afterthought."

The night before, *anticipate* what you are going to see.

As you get there the next day, *approach* the site with all the expectation you can muster, as if it is the only spot on earth that matters.

When you finally arrive, *acknowledge* its sacred presence.

After you leave, record your *afterthoughts* about what you experienced.

This book has arranged each site with these requirements in mind.

First, you are given a reading to *anticipate* where you are going. Read it at the end of the preceding day, then go to bed with one of its phrases ringing in your ears.

You then will find another reading for the next day. Use it for the ride or walk to the place in question. It allows you to *approach* the site with nothing else on your mind. Often it is a psalm or a prayer that pilgrims have used to approach this place for centuries.

When you finally arrive, you get a third reading, usually a blessing. Blessings are the Jewish route to the sacred. Say the blessing to *acknowledge* being there, and drink in the magic of the place. Let it become part of your being.

Then later on still, record your *afterthoughts*—for yourself and for posterity.

READING SEVENTEEN
Blessings!

Mostly, this is a book of blessings. Blessings are a brilliant mode of spiritual expression designed by the Rabbis some 2,000 years ago. They are now so integral to Jewish spirituality that they are taken for granted, even though they are the key to Judaism's uniqueness.

The Rabbis followed the psalmist's view that "The earth is God's and the fullness thereof, the world and they that dwell therein." God is therefore everywhere, apt to break in upon us at any moment—in the fullness of a spring blossom, the raw force of a thunderstorm or a memory in the march of time. Rather than let such moments pass unrecognized, the Rabbis outfitted Judaism with blessings, a simple but eloquent genre of appreciation for life's special moments.

Blessings are immediately recognizable by their form. You probably know some of them by heart but have never considered how unique to Judaism they are, and with what genius they were invented. They are usually one-liners that recur so frequently in Jewish prayers that most Jews memorize their opening formula without even meaning to:

בָּרוּךְ אַתָּה יְיָ אֱלֹהֵינוּ מֶלֶךְ הָעוֹלָם ....

Barukh atah Adonai Eloheinu melekh ha'olam ....

The usual word-for-word translation is, "Blessed art thou, Lord our God, King of the Universe. . . ." But it is often shortened to "Blessed is God. . . ." That is the way it appears in this book. Either way, the idea is that at moments that matter, we pause to acknowledge the presence of God.

That simple introductory formula is expanded to encompass the particular event we have in mind. We begin a meal, for instance, only after acknowledging God's gift of food in the first place (and, implicitly, the Rabbis say, by praying for food in abundance, some day, for all the world's hungry people).

בָּרוּךְ אַתָּה יְיָ אֱלֹהֵינוּ מֶלֶךְ הָעוֹלָם
הַמּוֹצִיא לֶחֶם מִן הָאָרֶץ.

Barukh atah Adonai, Eloheinu melekh ha'olam, hamotsi lechem min ha'aretz.

Blessed is God, who brings forth bread from the earth.

Similarly, when encountering a place where a miracle of history once occurred—maybe you should memorize this one; you will be using it a lot—we say:

בָּרוּךְ אַתָּה יְיָ אֱלֹהֵינוּ מֶלֶךְ הָעוֹלָם
שֶׁעָשָׂה נִסִּים לַאֲבוֹתֵינוּ בַּמָּקוֹם הַזֶּה.

Barukh atah Adonai, Eloheinu melekh ha'olam, she'asah nissim la'avoteinu bamakom hazeh.

Blessed is God, who performed miracles for our ancestors in this very place.

When Israel's poet laureate S. Y. Agnon went to Copenhagen to receive the Nobel Prize for literature, observers were surprised to find him conversing briefly with the Swedish monarch who presented him with the award. Careful rehearsal had impressed on the recipients the need to retain the strict formality of courtroom etiquette, whereby they were simply to march down the aisle, take the award, bow, and leave.

When questioned as to what he had said, Agnon explained, "I am a Jew. I have inherited many blessings from my ancestors, including one to be said in the presence of royalty. But I have never stood before a king or queen. Finally I got to say a blessing that has eluded me all these years, 'Blessed is God, who shares divine glory with earthly rulers.'"

Not all of us can be poets laureate or recipients of the Nobel Prize. But we all share Agnon's heritage of blessings, and visiting Israel gives us a chance to greet Israel's marvels with the same age-old formulas as Agnon drew upon to greet a modern-day monarch.

The most important part of this book is its blessings, a chance to get in touch with the sacred in an authentically Jewish way, inherited from 2,000 years of history. Reaching deep down into the collective memory of the Jewish people to find a genuine spiritual response to the sites of our ancient land is better than saying a simple, modern, succinct "Wow."

READING EIGHTEEN

A Pilgrim's Diary: Memories in the Making

Another Nobel Prize winner for literature, Isaac Bashevis Singer, is reputed to have said, "We Jews have many faults, but amnesia is not among them." A visit to Israel will convince you of the Jewish persistence of memory. We may be the people of the book, but our book of books is a record of what we choose to remember. Long before Americans were remembering the Alamo, we were taught to remember that we had been slaves in the land of Egypt. We light *yahrzeit* (memorial) candles to remember those who die. We say *Yizkor*, our memorial service, several times a year, and on Rosh Hashanah, we ask God, "Remember us for life."

Part of being made in God's image is this gift of memory. It is not clear, for instance, how much other forms of life can even do this. Beyond their inherited instincts, imprinted in their genetic code from millions of years of evolution, animals remember relatively little. Try training your pet dog to do a simple trick. You need a great deal of positive reinforcement. By contrast, humans revel in memory work. The reason is simple. We are, above all, meaning-making animals. And memory is how we find patterns from the past that make life meaningful.

The world strikes our senses, and we are immediately driven to interpret it: not simply for practical ends—animals do that too, deciding if this sound or that shadow means danger or opportunity—but as artistic constructs. Forest animals can analyze the shape of cloud formations to see if a storm is imminent; only human beings expect that the clouds will also reveal patterns, beauty, and design.

From the perspective of animals, the land of Israel is just so much sand, rock, and sunshine. For human beings, it can be much more. For Jews, it is more still. It is a land where our people met God, and where we hope to do the same.

A pilgrimage is an exercise in stretching your memory. If you emerge from the experience richer for it, it will be because you have become more richly human by being more fully Jewish. That is the point of the *Afterthought* section provided for each of the sites covered in this book.

To get the most from your journey, take the time and effort to sustain your capacity for memory. You will be adding your memories to those of the countless generations who came before you. As you stand on ancient ruins, or see the sun over the Mediterranean, or eat in a settlement where once there was only malarial swamp, you may find a million thoughts and emotions coursing through you. You will take pictures to savor the moment, as you should, but do not ask the pictures to do more than they can. They can make two-dimensional copies of three-dimensional experiences, but they can never reproduce what you felt at that moment, what you said in your heart you would always remember, what you promised to tell your children or grandchildren someday.

The essence of the spiritual life is keeping alive the deep-seated thoughts and feelings that rise to consciousness at such moments. If you let them slip away, they may never return. So write them down. Memory is partly what you draw from your past and partly what generations yet to come will inherit from you. Do your bit to sustain memory beyond yourself. Make your experience part of the Jewish People's heritage.

In the end, this is more than a guidebook. It is a pilgrim's diary, and you are the pilgrim. Enter your response to the sites you visit as memories in the making, and you will have them forever: for you and for those you love, this will be *your* contribution to the memory of this people that has never suffered from amnesia.

T'fillat Haderekh:
Prayers Before Leaving,
for Synagogue and Home

—————————— or ——————————

What to Say on the Eve of Leaving

I rejoiced when they said to me,
"Let us go to the house of God."

—Psalm 122:1

For the Shabbat Prior to Leaving

A Prayer for the Shabbat Table

Those leaving on pilgrimage to Israel during the week to come should recite the following, if possible, in the company of friends and family who are invited to share the moment of anticipation around the Shabbat table.

> *May the One who blessed our ancestors,*
> > *Abraham, Isaac, and Jacob,*
> > *Sarah, Rebekah, Rachel and Leah,*
> *Bless me and those with whom I travel,*
> *On this, our journey up to Israel.*
> *May we travel safely,*
> *And arrive in peace to the land that we hold dear,*
> > *the land that we call Zion.*
> *May we return to those we love*
> > *blessed in every undertaking*
> > *inspired and renewed by our People in our land.*
> *Amen.*

It is customary to collect written prayers to insert into the *Kotel*, the Wall, and token amounts of *tz'dakah* (charity) to leave with the poor in Israel (the usual amount is a dollar, but some give more). Explain to those around the table that you are happy to take any prayers that they write out and monetary gifts they leave with you. The former will be deposited in the cracks of the Wall, and the latter will be dispersed at your discretion to those who need it. Then say . . .

> *God make me a messenger for those I love.*
> *Let me carry their prayers as if they were my own,*

and leave them there, softly,
like bird's eggs, nesting in the crack of a wall,
awaiting the time for all they contain
to break out into joyous birth.
God grant me too
The merit to carry the means to Israel's redemption.
Until such time as we see the end of days,
God, make me a witness to history.
May I revel in its glories,
And relieve its pains.
In some small way, let this, my journey,
Awaken hope in those I love and those I barely know,
The people among whom I walk in the days ahead.

בָּרוּךְ אַתָּה יְיָ אֱלֹהֵינוּ מֶלֶךְ הָעוֹלָם עֹשֵׂה צְדָקוֹת.

Barukh atah Adonai Eloheinu melekh ha'olam,
oseh ts'dakot.

Blessed is God, for acts of kindness.

A Prayer for the Synagogue

People leaving on pilgrimage to Israel during the week to come are customarily given an *aliyah* in their synagogue, after which the following is recited by the rabbi or cantor on behalf of the congregation.

מִי שֶׁבֵּרַךְ אֲבוֹתֵינוּ,
אַבְרָהָם יִצְחָק וְיַעֲקֹב,
שָׂרָה, רִבְקָה, רָחֵל וְלֵאָה,
הוּא יְבָרֵךְ אֶת _____
הָעוֹמֵד / הָעוֹמֶדֶת לַעֲלוֹת
[יַחַד עִם מִשְׁפַּחְתּוֹ / מִשְׁפַּחְתָּה]
לְאֶרֶץ יִשְׂרָאֵל.
יְהִי רָצוֹן מִלְּפָנֶיךָ
שֶׁיִּסַּע / שֶׁתִּסַּע לְשָׁלוֹם,
וְשֶׁיַּגִּיעַ / וְשֶׁתַּגִּיעַ בְּשָׁלוֹם לְאֶרֶץ חֶמְדַּת לִבֵּנוּ,
לְאֶרֶץ צִיּוֹן.

יְהִי רָצוֹן מִלְפָנֶיךָ שֶׁיַּחֲזֹר/שֶׁתַּחֲזֹר אֵלֵינוּ
מְבֹרָךְ/מְבֹרֶכֶת בְּכָל מַעֲשָׂיו/מַעֲשֶׂיהָ,
מְחֻדָּשׁ/מְחֻדֶּשֶׁת מֵעַמֵּנוּ בִּמְדִינָתֵנוּ.

May the One who blessed our ancestors
  Abraham, Isaac and Jacob,
    Sarah, Rebekah, Rachel and Leah,
Bless_____
Who is about to ascend (with his/her family)
to the land of Israel.
May he/she travel there safely,
And arrive in peace to the land we hold dear,
  the land we call Zion.
May he/she return to us
  blessed in every undertaking
    inspired and renewed by our People in our land.
Tseitchem l'shalom, uvo'akhem l'shalom
We pray that you and all who go to Israel as you do,
May fly on angels' wings,
Transporting prayers of all this holy congregation
For life and peace.
To which we say . . . Amen!

How to Shape Sacred Time

or

How to Prepare While on the Way

For reading on the plane over to Israel.

You saw what I did . . .
how I carried you
on the wings of eagles.

—*Exodus 19:4*

Before your plane to Israel departs, recite *T'fillat Haderekh*, "Prayer for a Safe Journey" (p. 221). Then, during the flight, read the following.

A. Finding (and Using) What You Want

1. This Place Is Holy (Section Four)

The centerpiece of this book is Section Four, "This Place Is Holy." It is a register of places, arranged according to four geographic regions, north, south, east, and west, following God's promise to Abraham.

> God said to Abram, "Raise your eyes and look out from where you are, *tsafonah v'negbah v'kedmah v'ya-mah,* to the North and South, to the East and West, for I give all the land that you see to you and your ancestors forever" (Genesis 13:14–15).

The places are listed in the Table of Contents, as well as alphabetically in the Index.

The list includes the spiritual sites that you are most likely to visit. For each one, it provides opportunities to *anticipate, approach,* and *acknowledge* the site (see pp. 49–51). The pages for each place also have lots of empty space for you to record *afterthoughts,* your own spiritual diary of the memories in the making to which you will want to return from time to time, and that you will be able to share with those you love. (See pp. 53–54.)

Here are some tips on how to make the best use of the register of places.

- *Before traveling to any of the four geographic regions,* look through the Table of Contents for the places in that region to get a feel for the area as a whole.

- *Each night,* go over your itinerary for the next day and see if the places that you expect to visit are in the Index.

- *Anticipation:* Once you have located the page(s) where tomorrow's destination is found, spend some time the night before you go there reading the Anticipation section. It generally gives you a feel for the place so that you will appreciate it better when you get there.

- *Approach:* Think of places as having a *focus* and a *vicinity.* For your guests whom you invite over for dinner, for example, your house is the focus of their trip; your neighborhood is the vicinity. The Wall in Jerusalem is a focus; a large surrounding empty square from which the Wall can be seen but not yet experienced, is the vicinity. We naturally feel our adrenaline rise when we know we are in the *vicinity* and the *focus* is near.

    When you arrive at the vicinity, or in the car or bus on your way to the site, read the paragraph marked *Approach.* This is usually an evocative poem or reading, often from the Bible, the Talmud, or the writings of a pilgrim who came here before you. It will give you a spiritual sense of the place's ambiance.

- *Acknowledgment:* It is traditional to say blessings immediately prior to the experience for which the blessing exists, as a way of greeting the experience in question and integrating it into consciousness. The experience usually occurs when you come face to face with the *focus,* not just the general *vicinity* in which the focus is found. Each site's Acknowledgment section is preceded by a suggestion as to where the Acknowledgment prayer should be said. But you need not limit yourself to the suggestion. If you prefer, whenever you feel yourself to be at the *focus*—the spiritual center of the site—stop where you are, and acknowledge its presence with the section marked Acknowledgment.

- *Guide to Blessing:* There is no way to know for sure all the places you will visit, or the thoughts and emotions that any one of them will evoke within you. Also, some blessings and readings are intended for more than one place. Before the plane lands, therefore, look through the Guide to Blessing (Section Five). It contains special readings intended for more than a single place: for "a place of beauty," for instance, or "a place of prayer," and so on. You may want to use these blessings over and over again, as you go from place to place.

- *Time alone:* At every place, take some time to be alone with the site, your book, yourself and God. Formulate some reflections, reactions or observations to record later as your Afterthoughts.

- *Afterthoughts:* Do not delay writing your thoughts down. You will be amazed how quickly you forget what you wanted to say when the experience was fresh in your mind.

2. The Guide to Blessing (Section Five)

Places are fixed in space. We have the luxury of traveling back and forth among them, visiting, revisiting, scheduling and anticipating. Time, on the other hand, comes but once, and is gone forever after. We try to plan it, but we never know exactly what the next moment may bring.

You will know well in advance, therefore, what places you can expect to visit, but you will never know for sure what opportunities you will have to greet a special moment that will come with fleeting immediacy and then vanish.

On one of my trips to Israel, for instance, I found myself in a Roman Catholic retreat house where I had been invited to lecture just before and after the holiday of Shavuot. Knowing that Shavuot is a pilgrim festival on which the Torah prescribes traveling to Jerusalem to eat and celebrate, I asked an Israeli acquaintance with a car to do me the favor of stopping at a bakery along the way to buy some pastry. Lunch hour in the retreat house was normally spent eating together, and time was allotted for announcements by tour guides, leaders of study expeditions, and the like. With some 100 guests from around the world gathered around me, none of whom I knew personally, I rose and invited everyone to share in my great joy at being able to fulfill this biblical commandment to be in Jerusalem at the time of the pilgrimage festival and to eat of the sweetness of the land. One by one, people came forward as their own lunch ended to request a piece of my pastry. As they ate, some thanked me, some thanked God, some offered me blessings, some just smiled, but all looked deeply into my eyes knowing that a precious moment had passed among us.

The Guide to Blessing is your reference to those special moments that tend to come some time during everyone's pilgrimage. I mean such things as catching a desert flower in full bloom, or standing in a place where miraculous events transpired once upon a time. These are awe-inspiring episodes of the ordinary, the burning bushes of our time, and Jewish tradition provides blessings for them.

You will want to know in advance what these blessings are or, at least, that a blessing exists, since the event in question may occur so unexpectedly that you will not have much time to find out what Jewish tradition provides for you to say. The Guide to Blessing therefore provides blessings for "generic" occasions. *Before your plane lands, spend some time with this section so that you have some idea of the blessings.* When you find yourself at a spot where you are moved to say a blessing, you may recall that it exists, and be able to look it up in time to use it.

The pages in Section Five contain suggestions as to where some of these time-bound blessings might be said. But these are only suggestions. Who knows when the right opportunity will arise? Be prepared! Do not let sacred moments pass. They never come again.

3. A Meal in Jerusalem (Section Six)

A special section is allotted to the single experience that has most typified a Jewish pilgrimage to Israel: sharing a meal of thanksgiving and celebration on sacred soil. It is suggested for Jerusalem, since Torah itself commands us to go there and eat with friends or family in the confines of the city that has consistently represented the final goal of every pilgrim's dream. In Second Temple times, a regular stream of visitors came from all around to do just that.

Section Six therefore provides a set of mealtime prayers, including a *Birkat Hamazon,* Grace after Meals. The version of blessings included is not entirely the same as the one you may be used to using back home, because it comes directly out of the body of ancient prayers found in the Cairo *Genizah*. They are part of the liturgy used by Jews in *Eretz Yisrael* before they fled from the Crusaders in 1099. By the time they returned, often several generations later, they had exchanged their ancient way of prayer for the customs they had discovered in the Diaspora. Only at the beginning of the twentieth century did archeologists discover manuscripts of their original prayers buried in the sands of time.

Who would have believed, when our ancestors fled from the approaching Crusaders, that their descendants would return some day to our land and make their prayers our own? The physical bodies of those Jews may have perished, but their spirit has not. When you say these prayers, you will be saying words that have not been said for 1,000 years.

It has always been a mitzvah of the highest order for pilgrims to eat in Jerusalem, thereby celebrating their homecoming and thanking God for the bounty available to them. Plan, therefore, at least one meal together as a group, and recapture as your own the prayers that Jews recited when they lived in Israel long ago.

4. Afterward: Keeping a Journal as Memories in the Making

Sections Four (This Place Is Holy) and Five (Guide to Blessing) provide space in which to record your response to where you have been and what you have done. Journal writing is a lost art. Most of us use the phone for personal calls, and limit letter writing to business matters. Our most profound and personal thoughts often pass fleetingly through our minds, and then get strangled before emerging full-blown in all their glory. But the Rabbis say that the very air of *Eretz Yisrael* makes us wise. This, after all, is the land of the prophets and judges of Israel, the men and women who were seized by inspiration that they never expected. You may be surprised to discover how deep your own thoughts are.

Take fifteen minutes each night to write them down, *even if they do not seem deep at the time.* You may feel that you have nothing to say, but you do. To begin with, your notes will help you remember what to tell the folks back home.

But in addition, think how grateful you would be if you could have a diary that your grandparents had composed. Now is your chance to keep a diary for people who come after you.

Record how you felt. Or, if you like, compose a poem, draw a picture, or write your own prayer. Do something with your thoughts, and you will have a memento more precious than any souvenir you might buy: a journal of your own interior landscape that you might never have known you had, something to read and reread back home, a diary to pass on to posterity.

B. The Jewish Dimension

1. Blessings

As you discovered in your preparatory reading (pp. 51–53), the most important part of this book are the blessings for the times you come face to face with the sites and history of Israel. To appreciate what you are saying, you need to know a little more about where the blessings come from.

Like *T'fillat Haderekh*, the prayer for a safe journey, many of the blessings come directly from our standard prayer book, the *Siddur*. Others never made it to the *Siddur*, but can be found buried in ancient texts like the Talmud, codified for all time by the sages who set Judaism on its course centuries ago. Others never even made it to the Talmud. Our "official" Jewish books, the Talmud included, are only part of the Jewish heritage. We have, in addition, unofficial records, like diaries of pilgrims such as you, or writings by pious men and women of many eras whose words remained marginal to the official collection of rabbinic literature, but have been rediscovered by scholars in our time.

Of special relevance is the magnificent cache of ancient documents that I mentioned briefly above: the Cairo *Genizah*, with its spiritual heritage of *Eretz Yisrael* from Crusader times. When the Crusader armies from France, England and Germany arrived in Israel in 1099, they conquered the land, and established what they called the Latin Kingdom of Jerusalem. Most Jews fled or were expelled, but they returned about a century later, when the kingdom finally fell. In the interim, their native spiritual legacy, born of Jewish life in Israel for almost 1,000 years, was lost in the dust of time.

At the turn of this century, archaeologists exploring an old synagogue in Cairo, Egypt, stumbled upon a whole library of documents, miraculously saved by the arid climate there. To their surprise, the cache was a paper trail of Jewish life before and after the Crusaders arrived, and among its tatters of pages piled knee deep all over the floor were prayers from the community that the Crusaders expelled. They had apparently been taken to Egypt, where they had been relegated to museum-like status and forgotten. This book reproduces some of those fragments, as well as whatever else we know about the spiritual life of Jews in Israel 1,000 years ago.

In our time, we have recovered the physical heritage of the land. We have rebuilt it, making it again our own. So too, with this book, we recover the blessings and prayers that our forebears in Israel used to say over 1,000 years ago. We say again these, their prayers, in Israel, their land, affirming that both land and prayers are ours as well.

2. Endnotes for Depth

Yes, there are endnotes, but not the scholarly kind. Usually they tell you where the blessings are from. Make sure to use them to appreciate what you are saying.[1]

C. The Personal Dimension

1. Know Your Trip

Whether you are traveling by yourself or in a group, you will have to find time to be alone with the places you visit rather than in the midst of busy crowds listening to historical lectures on what you are seeing. You should do the following:

- You can easily manage the Anticipation and Approach parts of your pilgrimage. Do these as indicated, reading the Anticipation the night before and the Approach while traveling to the place in question.

- The problem comes with the Acknowledgment. If you

are traveling as part of a group, it may not occur to anyone else to stop and say a blessing, and you will not be given time to thumb through this book to find what you want while everyone else continues on their way touring. You will therefore have to know in advance what blessing to say. Use a bookmark to have your book ready for the moment you arrive.

- As soon as you arrive at the place's focus, and feel the sense of its presence, open your book and stop to say your blessing.

- *Take your time; do it right; treat your spiritual impulses seriously.* Above all, *don't be shy.* You have the right to go off by yourself (within the bounds of safety), to linger behind briefly, or to ask the rest of your group to wait a moment until the impact of the event has been fully realized. The apt expression here is *derekh eretz*, the Jewish value of "respect for others." Spirituality is often intensely personal, so you should not expect that everyone will want to do exactly what you do or to take as much time doing it. Within the bounds of *derekh eretz*, however, the others will appreciate your taking these spiritual moments seriously, even if this means asking them to wait silently for the minute it takes to finish the page you are on, close your eyes to meditate, or open your eyes to let a tear flow undisturbed. (They would not think twice about asking you to wait a minute while they take another picture, or ask another question of the guide.) Spirituality is contagious; empower yourself to appreciate the sacred, and you will empower those with you to do the same.

You will then be ready to listen to your guide or to continue on the way along with the others. Most tours give you some private time after the official *"schpiel"* is over. Other people will use it to ask questions or just to wander around. This is a wonderful chance to be alone and think through what you may want to record as an Afterthought in your diary after you leave.

If you are on a tour or with a group in which everyone is using this book, you have the chance to organize each day to get the most out of the places you visit. You can pause together as a group, as everyone approaches and acknowledges the sites.

Remember that some places (especially Jerusalem) have more than one site where a blessing is in order. Sacred sites tend to cluster together in space the way holy days do in time. Like the High Holy Days of Rosh Hashanah and Yom Kippur, Israel is a High Holy Place, within which particular locations loom especially rich in the presence of the holy. Any given place may call for more than one blessing. One site may appear in This Place is Holy (Section Four); another may not, but it may nonetheless evoke a blessing from the Guide to Blessing (Section Five). Do not feel that you have to hurry. Spend the time it takes to see and to say whatever the spiritual moments prompt.

2. Overcome Your Jewish Education

You may be struck in Israel at how little you know about Judaism. Worse yet, you may discover that the Jewish schooling of your youth actually discouraged the experience of the spiritual, to the point where you are hesitant about giving yourself over to the sacredness of Israel. Treating it as history is easy. But as the place of God? Well. . . .

Up above, I discussed the dilemma you may have if you are on a tour with strangers, and you are the only person with this book. But oddly enough, people are usually least shy with strangers. It may be the people we know and love most whom we are afraid to startle with our new-found spiritual impulses. Parents who are not accustomed to saying prayers except in congregational settings are often afraid to pray in front of their children, to the point where they cannot get themselves to do so—in which case, the children lose almost as much as their parents do. No matter what formal Jewish education you have given your children, you will find that it is less powerful in guaranteeing their Jewish future than the example you set yourself; children are moved by the experience of parents who are willing to stumble through an unfamiliar prayer or two, rather than feign cool detachment in the face of what matters most. Some of us are afraid even to put our arm around the people we love, lest we cry publicly, or they get a glimpse of the softness we have hidden for so long inside our normal efficient exterior.

Others still will concede that children need spiritual models, but will merely condescend to the kids, never open themselves up to the experience of the sacred for their own sake as adults—not publicly, anyway.

Avoid the mistake of retaining your cool. Whenever you use this book, make a point of doing so without embarrassment. If you want to, go off a few steps to be alone. Alone does not mean lonely, and you may find the experience of being alone with your thoughts and prayers of inestimable value. If the thought strikes you, ask someone you know to say "Amen!" after your blessing. You would ask them to take your picture, wouldn't you? Saying "Amen" takes a lot less time and is much easier. If you are with someone you love, you might even ask them to say the blessing with you, or just to hold your hand while you do so.

3. Be Creative

It never fails to amaze me how rational and competent adults, who organize families, care for children, attend to crises, and run businesses, somehow manage to revert to infancy when faced with religion. Our synagogues have often reduced us to passive observers or lemming-like followers of whatever the experts say and do. That wasn't the way the Rabbis of old meant things to turn out.

Once upon a time, there was no printing press, not even paper on which to scribble notes. Unable to have a handy pocket-size prayer book around, people were encouraged to master the *art* of saying their own blessings, more than the rote practice of repeating the precise wording of blessings that other people had already made up. To be sure, we now have both paper and printing technology, so we can have in hand the age-old blessings made doubly precious by the very fact that thirty generations and more have said them. But we have every right to make up new ones ourselves.

This is, admittedly, a liberal approach to Jewish tradition. Rabbis living after the year 1000 tended to use the blessings that were already available from earlier rabbinic literature, so that the codes of Jewish law prohibit inventing new blessings for occasions that the Talmud never envisioned. People who follow Jewish law in its full and literal detail will hesitate to compose blessings they think Jewish law prohibits.

We know, however, that even after the year 1000, many Jews did, in practice, write their own blessings. And even those who did not write actual blessings complete with the formal introductory formula, "*Barukh atah Adonai Eloheinu melekh ha'olam*," did not hesitate to write prayers in freely composed prose or poetry.

Still, in practice, we rarely see new blessings still being composed today, and it cannot be denied that Jewish law (*halakhah*) prohibits the use of made-up blessings, for fear that by using blessings loosely, we may be taking God's name in vain. On the other hand, we are encouraged to recognize God in all we do. Liberally minded Jews may prefer to follow the precedent of people in the Middle Ages who wrote new blessings despite the technical prohibition against them, on the grounds that saying blessings is central to Jewish spirituality. They may argue that even the Talmud would allow them to do so in this day and age. Most Orthodox (and some Conservative) authorities, however, will permit new blessings only if the phrase that introduces them is shortened to omit God's name and the reference to God's rulership. Instead of saying the whole phrase, "*Barukh atah Adonai Eloheinu melekh ha'olam*" ("Blessed are You, Adonai our God, ruler of the world . . .") they advocate saying only "*Barukh atah*" ("Blessed are You"), or using the English translation alone.

In sum:

- Decide what your own parameters are. But whatever you do, do not feel that you must limit yourself to what you find in the pages here.

- If you want to make up blessings, note how easy it is; just say:

בָּרוּךְ אַתָּה יְיָ אֱלֹהֵינוּ מֶלֶךְ הָעוֹלָם

or

בָּרוּךְ אַתָּה

Barukh atah Adonai Eloheinu melekh ha'olam
or
Barukh atah

Blessed is God who . . . (add whatever seems right to you).

4. The Sacred and the Everyday

It has often been said that Judaism is a religion of the everyday. It is not that we are intent on transforming the everyday into the sacred. It is that the sacred exists around every ordinary bend in life's journey. Our daily prayer acknowledging the miracles of God, for instance, does not specify the spectacular instances of the hand of God. Instead, you find mention of "Your miracles which are with us daily, the wonders and goodness that occur all the time—morning, noon and night." On the great occasions that recollect God's miracles—Passover, for instance—we say a set of psalms called the *Hallel*, prayers of gratitude and awe at what God has done. But every day begins with such a set of prayers; the ordinary morning service starts with a lengthy section called *Hallel Sheb'khol Yom*—the Daily *Hallel*.

Jews are trained to look for God in ordinary places: faces on the street, blossoms on a tree, a simple loaf of bread. Remember Elijah as he heads to the wilderness to find God:

> Then, lo, the Lord passed by. There was a great and mighty wind, splitting mountains and shattering rocks by the power of the Lord. But the Lord was not in the wind. After the wind, an earthquake; but the Lord was not in the earthquake. After the earthquake, fire; but the Lord was not in the fire. And after the fire—a still, small voice (1 Kings 18:11–12).

Blessings are our own still small voice, the best approximation we have to being Godlike ourselves. They are an act of creation, that convert the ordinary into the extraordinary, not because they are a kind of verbal alchemy turning leaden experience into gold, but because they reveal the sacred in the everyday.

Here is your first blessing. Try saying it now:

בָּרוּךְ אַתָּה יְיָ אֱלֹהֵינוּ מֶלֶךְ הָעוֹלָם
הַמֵּכִין מִצְעֲדֵי גָבֶר.

*Barukh atah Adonai Eloheinu melekh ha'olam,
hameichin mitsadei gaver.*

Blessed is God who sets us firmly upon our way.[2]

5. Prayers for Arrival

Anticipation

(To be recited shortly before landing.)

I've seen the old-time films of how they kiss the ground,
Those old-time Jews unblemished by sophistication.
As for me, well, I'll just look around, unexcited-like,
Cool as a cucumber.
(Or maybe as a m'lah-f'foan, *as they call cucumbers*
  here.)
This is just an airport where they lose your bags the same
  as any place on earth,
But in Hebrew.
I've heard the tales of Jews who burst out crying on these
  shores,
Middle-aged men from the Middle Ages, mostly,
Who had a thing for tears, I guess—
It was a wailing wall, back then, where they cried each
  day at sunrise and at sunset,
And watched and waited for the Ninth of Av, with special
  joy, for all I know,
Because they could cry more then.
But as for me, well, thank you, I don't cry a lot,
Not even in Jerusalem,
Let alone in Tel Aviv, where (after all)
People plod to work, smoke cigarettes, drink Coca Cola
(Koa-kah koa-lah, as they call it here—
Who says I can't speak Hebrew?)
But then again, I've never really come like this,
Never stood here, all alone with just my jet-lagged
  thoughts
On what I should be careful not to do,
In case someone is watching.
Who doesn't wonder what it was like
To embrace the ground
And steal at least a single kiss,
From the dust of Israel's past,
The way they did
When pre-jet props used runways made of smoothed-out
  sacred soil, instead of tarmac?

בָּרוּךְ אַתָּה יְיָ אֱלֹהֵינוּ מֶלֶךְ הָעוֹלָם מְכוֹפֵף זְקוּפִים.

*Barukh atah Adonai Eloheinu melekh ha'olam,
m'khofef z'kufim.*

Blessed is God, who lets us fall upon our knees.[3]

Acknowledgment

1. On arriving safely
(To be said as the plane comes to a stop.)

בָּרוּךְ אַתָּה יְיָ אֱלֹהֵינוּ מֶלֶךְ הָעוֹלָם
הַגּוֹמֵל לְחַיָּבִים טוֹבוֹת שֶׁגְּמָלַנִי כָּל טוֹב.

*Barukh atah Adonai Eloheinu melekh ha'olam,
hagomel l'chayavim tovot sheg'malani kol tov.*

Blessed is God, who does favors even for the un-deserving, and has treated me so kindly.[4]

2. For the road from the airport to Jerusalem . . .

(The airport is near the Mediterranean coast. But very shortly, the car taking you to Jerusalem will turn inland, and then, just short of the city, you begin to climb a long road upward—up to the sacred center of the Jewish universe! If you can, ask your driver to stop along the way, perhaps near the rusted remains of the armored vehicles that were left as visible reminders of the fight for independence in 1948. Then read the following:)

On the Road to Jerusalem

The drivers of these vehicles were not pilgrims, not like us. Nor were they tourists. They were warriors with guns, not cameras. It was 1948, and Jerusalem was surrounded by enemy troops intent on strangling the city into submission. Its survival depended on a daily convoy carrying food up what was then a narrow mountain road guarded on both sides by enemy fire. Slowly but inexorably, the amount of food that got through tailed off to a fraction of what was needed, so in March, the Haganah mounted a large convoy of forty trucks. Guarded in the front and rear by armored vehicles, this was a last-ditch attempt to break through the siege with flour, canned goods, and even oranges, for the 100,000 Jerusalemites who were completely cut off from all communication with the outside world.

Arab intelligence learned of the plan in time to mount an ambush. Stones that looked like an ordinary road block were outfitted with land mines that would explode when the convoy's leading vehicles pushed through. The trucks carrying food would then be trapped behind the metal debris and human remains from the lead vehicles, easy targets for the hand grenades that hidden soldiers carried on both sides of the road.

The attack went as planned. Hand grenades destroyed the trucks, forcing their drivers out onto the road. There they were met with bullets fired by Arab villagers from all along the road who had joined the regular troops in anticipated victory. What was left of the convoy managed to turn around or back down the hill to safety. But nineteen vehicles, roughly half of those which began the journey, were destroyed, their drivers and occupants killed. To this day, their rusted hulks have been left in sight, that all who enter Jerusalem may not take their journey here for granted.

From *Psalm 25—Tanks and Planes Are Not the True Salvation* by Danny Siegel

O Lord
We are chosen,
but weary of the tear soaked pages
of our history.

We ask nothing of You, Lord,
but opportunities to raise
carnations in the Negev
and a crop of cinnamon
in Galilee.

(Facing Jerusalem at the top of the mountain road, add:)

עוֹד יִשָּׁמַע   *Od yishama*

בְּעָרֵי יְהוּדָה   *b'arei y'hudah*

וּבְחוּצוֹת יְרוּשָׁלַיִם   *uv'chutsot y'rushalayim*

קוֹל שָׂשׂוֹן וְקוֹל שִׂמְחָה,   *kol sason v'kol simchah*

קוֹל חָתָן וְקוֹל כַּלָּה.   *kol chatan v'kol kallah*

In the cities of Judah
And the courtyards of Jerusalem,
Let only this be heard:
    the sound of joy and happiness,
    weddings on every corner.[5]

בָּרוּךְ אַתָּה יְיָ אֱלֹהֵי דָוִד בּוֹנֶה יְרוּשָׁלָיִם.

Barukh atah Adonai, Elohei david, boneh y'rushalayim.

Blessed is the God of David, who builds up Jerusalem.[6]

3. *For arriving at your destination in Jerusalem:*

בָּרוּךְ אַתָּה יְיָ אֱלֹהֵינוּ מֶלֶךְ הָעוֹלָם
שֶׁהֶחֱיָנוּ וְקִיְּמָנוּ וְהִגִּיעָנוּ לַזְּמַן הַזֶּה.

Barukh atah Adonai Eloheinu melekh ha'olam, shehecheyanu v'kiy'manu v'higiyanu lazman hazeh.

Blessed is God for granting us life, for sustaining us, and for bringing us to this moment.

4. *Before retiring for the first night in Israel*
(The following may be said alone, but is intended, preferably, for the whole group to say together before dispersing for the night.)

Oh God,
How far we've traveled, just for this,
To be just here,
Precisely here, at this most sacred place,
Exactly now, at this most sacred time

for which we have devoutly hoped—and worked—and waited.
And so we pray for every happy circumstance that you may bless us with.
Help us cling dearly to this moment of our lives,
To hold it softly in our hands, and then, to fit it firmly in its place in memory.
Help us in the days ahead
To wend our way through history.
Help us hear the echo of the words heard by prophets,
Of dry bones rising or of David's wild dance on his way to Jerusalem.
As we go from place to place
May we go from strength to strength,
And find the words to offer silent prayers to You
Of time gone by, or yet to come,
Assured by the knowledge
That moments truly marked by prayer can never vanish in the wind.

בָּרוּךְ אַתָּה יְיָ הַמְחַדֵּשׁ יָמֵינוּ כְּקֶדֶם.

Barukh atah Adonai, ham'chadesh yameinu k'kedem.

Blessed is God, who renews our days as of old.[7]

This Place Is Holy

— or —

What to Say at Specific Places

God said to Abram, "Raise your eyes
and look out from where you are,
tsafonah v'negbah v'kedmah v'yamah,
to the north and south, to the east and
west, for I give all the land that you see
to you and your ancestors forever."

—*Genesis 13:14–15*

THE GALIL:
"Tsafonah—to the North"

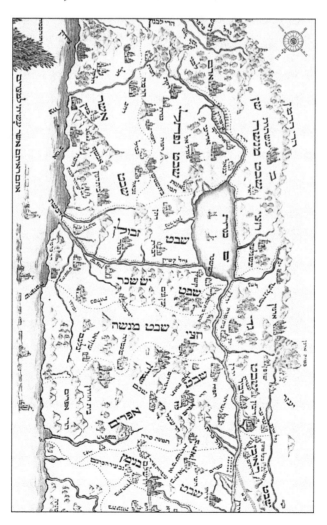

Deganya, Kibbutz in the Galil, Or Cemetery of Chalutzim (Pioneers) at the Kinneret (Sea of Galilee)

You shall eat of the labor of your hands.

—Psalm 128:2

Anticipation

Visit the *kibbutzim* up north around the *Kinneret,* especially Deganya (if you can) or go to the cemetery where the air is thick with memories of the *chalutzim*, the pioneers, whose legendary exploits and not-so-legendary labor created Israel out of nothing. Once this was mostly malaria-infested swampland. Now it is lush farmland. Kibbutz Deganya is the grandfather of the Kibbutz Movement, alive still with memories of A. D. Gordon (1856–1922) who gave modern Israel its ideology of sacred labor, and of Rachel Blaustein (1890–1931), "a young delicate girl from Russia," as Golda Meir remembered her, both a poet and a worker.

Gordon actually made aliyah alone, bringing his wife and daughter only five years later. Though he had never done an ounce of manual labor in his life, he plunged into backbreaking fieldwork in the vineyards and orange groves, contracted malaria, nearly died of starvation, but through it all, developed a theory of "the religion of labor."

Rachel (as she signed her poetry) came from Russia, fell under the spell of Gordon's revolutionary mysticism of labor, and returned briefly to France to study agriculture. Her education completed, she was forced to wait out World War I in Russia, where she taught children to make aliyah as she herself intended to do as soon as the war ended. Once in Israel, however, Rachel found that she had contracted tuberculosis, and simply could not work the land she loved so well. The world is grateful for her poetry now, but as Golda Meir, concludes, "This was her sorrow: that she could not do physical work."

The poetry of Israel echoes with the ideal of work that was so central to the psyche of the early immigrants, especially those from the Second and Third Aliyah, and who established the labor movement and the *kibbutzim*.[1] The religious love-affair they had with physical labor comes through clearly in the poem you will read tomorrow, by Abraham Shlonsky. Shlonsky a Ukrainian Jew, made aliyah in 1921. When not writing poetry, he worked on a construction gang and described himself as the "road-paving poet of Israel."

Approach

From the Writings of A.D. Gordon

I awake with a start and shake off that life that was over me and within me. I commence all things anew. I begin at the beginning. The first thing that opens my heart to a life such as I have not yet known is work. Not work for a livelihood, not work in obedience to a command, but work upon which a new light shines. This work, which I see is a part of life, one of life's deepest roots. So I work....

As I keep working, suffering, there is no drop of my blood, no ounce of my strength or intellect, which perishes uselessly. For every drop of blood is a spark of fire, and every ounce of strength or intellect is a spark of light to my soul which is being regenerated.... Our claim to the Land rests on whatever the Land or its life gains through our labor....We seek life, nothing more or less, our own life, from our own life-source, from the nature of the Land....We come to the Land to be imbedded in its natural soil from which we were uprooted, through our roots to draw sustenance from the earth, through our leaves to breathe in nourishment from the winds and from the creative power that lies in the rays of light.

At times you imagine that you too are taking root in the soil that you are digging; like all that is growing around, you are nurtured by the light of the sun's rays with food from heaven. You feel that you too live a life in common with the tiniest blade of grass, with each flower, each tree; that you live deeply in the heart of nature, rising up from it all and growing straight up into the expanse of the world . . . .

If we do not till the soil with our own hands, the soil will not be ours—the Land will not be ours, and we will not be the People of the Land. Even here we shall be aliens, just as in the lands of the Diaspora where, too, there are Jews who rent land, who buy fields, gardens, and orchards, but who traffic in the fruit and labor of others. . . . We cannot deceive ourselves much longer in the belief that investing money in business, parceling out work, and superintending affairs constitutes the essence of labor, the essence of such national creativity as will give us title to the Land.

One must first of all abandon the ordinary point of view: that which seemed to be the essentials of life, the pleasantness of life, the why and wherefore of life. It is useless to search for a new life, unless one's attitude toward life is transformed. A new life predicates a new zest for life. Palestine is more than a worn-out holiday costume, more than a means for an economic existence, more than a kind of business enterprise. We should judge it by the standard reserved for our ancient dream: redemption.[2]

Acknowledgment

(To be said, perhaps, in the fields of a kibbutz.)

Toil, Abraham Shlonsky

Dress me, good mother, in a robe of many colors.
Lead me at dawn to work.

My land is wrapped in light, as in a tallit.
The houses stand out like t'fillin boxes.
The roads, paved by hand, stream out like t'fillin
   straps.

Here the lovely city davens Shacharit to its creator.
And among its creators is your son, Abraham,
A road-building poet in Israel.

At evening twilight, father returns from his labor,
And whispers pleasantly, as if in prayer,
Haben yakir li Avraham[3]
Abraham is a dear son to me;
skin, sinews, and bones.
Hallelujah!

Dress me, good mother, in a robe of many colors.
Lead me at dawn to work.

בָּרוּךְ אַתָּה יְיָ אֱלֹהֵינוּ מֶלֶךְ הָעוֹלָם
הַמְכוֹנֵן מַעֲשֵׂי יָדֵינוּ.

Barukh atah Adonai Eloheinu melekh ha'olam,
ham'khonen ma'aseh yadeinu.

Blessed is God, who establishes the work of our
hands.[4]

(If you have an opportunity to eat at the kibbutz, see special
prayers for the occasion, p. 215.)

Afterthoughts

Jezreel Valley

I love you, I love every tree we planted,
every clod of this earth.

—*Pioneering founder of the valley,*
Manya Shochat, on her death bed

Anticipation

The Jezreel is Israel's largest inland valley, connecting east to west just south of the northland called the Galil. The biblical judge, Gideon, selected his troops in the spring of Harod (now a national park area) and at nearby En Dor (now a kibbutz), King Saul consulted a soothsayer before fighting his last battle on Mount Gilboa, which dominates the valley's southern rim. Pompey passed through in 63 B.C.E., building up Bet Shean, still the site of a magnificent Roman ampitheatre, and Napoleon followed him some 1,800 years later. The valley returned to Jewish hands with the establishment of the pioneer settlement of Merchavia in 1911.

The valley is home to famous mothers in Israel. Here Deborah the prophet subdued the Canaanites with the help of Ya'el, whom the Bible calls, "most blessed of women" for her military valor. Modern times produced Manya Shochat, a member of the pioneering group known as *Hashomer*, "The Watchers." Manya's biographer draws a vivid picture of the early years.

"A feeling of wonderment filled Manya as she watched her friends who first furrowed the land of the valley. From that moment in time, the valley was theirs. Manya participated in its colonization; its glorious moments as well as its times of threat, ceaselessly concerning herself with her friends in their ramshackle huts. The *Hashomer* members settled that land with superhuman self-sacrifice. Their first dwellings were of clay, only windowless huts, crawling with mice. Near them was a communal oven. Later on shacks were constructed and the place was renamed Merchavia."

Among other things, Manya served as treasurer. A 1911 letter back home to the Lovers of Zion foundation in Russia gives you a sense of just how tenuous the whole enterprise was.

"In response to your telegram, we are sending you a short analysis of *Hashomer*—about its meteoric rise, its multiple needs, and about the urgent requirement to set up a foundation which will free us from our constant supplications to the government. We will speak more of this in the future but for now, we will address the issue of how vital these 2,000 francs are for us, which we entreat you to wire us immediately. From the money which *Hashomer* received this year, we have the following balance:

Surety fund	Fr 4,000
Arms	Fr 1,400
Assistance Fund	Fr 1,300
11 horses	Fr 30,000

(One horse was shot in an Arab attack.)"

You can still visit any or all of these places. When you do, cast your eyes around the valley to remember the sacrifice that went into it—from Deborah to Manya, a period spanning 3,000 years of history.

Approach

The Harshness of the Pioneer Years,
by Anna Shochat, Manya's daughter

One of the central things was work and hard labor. To stand on your own, to work, to earn a living, to help others and to be a working laboring group. As children we practically did not learn, just worked, beginning from the age of five, from six in the morning. I do not remember vacation at all, only work. We, the children, were responsible for the sheep. We would milk the goats at ten and four and in between took them to graze. We could never go far because we had to get back for milking. We also did seasonal work, cleaning and threshing and shepherding—and always barefoot.

Another important tenet was loyalty. Not to inform and not to tell our friends. There were weapons, and we heard many stories that if they catch you and beat you, you must stand firm in the tortures and not tell. . . . We spent entire nights in the storehouse cleaning the bullets and shining them, removing the rust and making piles and piles. . . . We learned to handle weapons at the age of eleven, to dismantle and assemble rifles. Then there were exercises with guns, like taking them apart in the dark with our eyes closed. We practiced in the hayloft, but there was another special place, a secret place that we did not even dare to say its name out loud. Secrecy and loyalty were holy values. And this loyalty, this unwillingness ever to inform on a friend extended itself into also being always ready to help others.

We, the children of the kibbutz, grew up in two houses, six–seven to a room. There weren't enough beds, and we would sleep four in a bed. I still remember sleeping four in a bed head to toe, and we would remove the thorns from each other's feet because we were always barefoot.

I saw my mother cry once. I was ill with typhus. I was eleven years old. The fever kept going up. At first they thought I had malaria. I had six attacks. I remember lying there. They came in to take my temperature. The thermometer was in my hand, not even under my arm and the temperature was 42°C [over 105°F]. I was delirious, and they put ice on my body and the ice kept melting. I remember my mother sitting there with tears running down her face. I felt myself passing away, but somehow, I mustered up some strength and survived.

Many have asked what I did after four o'clock when all the children went to their parents. I had nowhere to go. I felt that I had nothing, that I was all alone. I pitied myself, but never really gave it serious thought. Mixed up with my feelings of not being good enough was the concept of the homeland. And my parents carried the burden of the homeland relentlessly on their backs. Once during one of the festivals, Ben-Gurion asked me something about my parents, and I told him that I was an orphan. I don't know how those words escaped, but he got angry and said that I should not dare speak like that again, that thanks to my parents, the settlement exists.[5]

Acknowledgment

(To be recited while standing in the valley, looking up at the surrounding mountains.)

The Song of Deborah, Judges 5:3, 7

אָנֹכִי לַיהוה אָנֹכִי אָשִׁירָה,
אֲזַמֵּר לַיהוה אֱלֹהֵי יִשְׂרָאֵל.
חָדְלוּ פְרָזוֹן,
בְּיִשְׂרָאֵל חָדֵלּוּ,
עַד שַׁקַּמְתִּי דְּבוֹרָה,
שַׁקַּמְתִּי אֵם בְּיִשְׂרָאֵל.

I will sing to the Lord
Will hymn the Lord the God of Israel. . . .
Deliverance ceased,
Ceased in Israel,
Until you arose, Deborah,
You arose a mother in Israel.

בָּרוּךְ אַתָּה יְיָ עוֹשֵׂה אִמָּהוֹת בְּיִשְׂרָאֵל.

Barukh atah Adonai, oseh imahot b'yisrael

Blessed is God, who establishes mothers in Israel.

Afterthoughts

Safed

Hin'ni mukhan um'zuman l'taken olam.
Here I am ready and prepared to make the world whole again.

—Based on the thought of Isaac Luria,
the Holy Ari of blessed memory[6]

Anticipation

Once commonly despised as superstitious nonsense, the Kabbalah has come into its own as a source of wisdom, deep beyond measure. If you spend one day in Safed, the home of Kabbalah, you will know why.

The narrow streets and alleyways seem to wind automatically to the synagogue of Rabbi Isaac Luria, known to posterity as the Ari, "the Lion," and also an acronym for Adoneino Rabbi Yitzchak, "Our master, Rabbi Isaac." He was the most influential genius of the many seers and sages who once walked these streets. They came mostly from Spain, remnants of the inquisition and expulsion, seeking answers to the chaos of their lives. They carried with them the *Zohar*, a thirteenth-century work of mystical meaning. The Ari and his circle proclaimed that a divine presence inhabits even the broken universe of tragedy and evil, awaiting the good work of human beings to mend the world. In the eighteenth century, this doctrine was adopted and expanded in Chasidism, and has recently reemerged as a modern mystical revival, the same search for meaning that haunted the Ari and his generation.

Across from the synagogue sits a cemetery considered by many to be the third most sacred site in all of Israel, just short of Jerusalem's *Kotel* and Temple mount, and perhaps Hebron. You will find your way down the stairs to the two large tombstones that dominate the old grave sites. One marks the resting place of the Ari himself; the other of Solomon Alkabetz, the author of the most famous synagogue Shabbat poem of all time: *L'kha Dodi,* "Come, my beloved to meet the [Shabbat] bride . . ."

Approach

From *The Pious Customs of Isaac Luria*[7]

1. The most important of all worthy traits consists in an individual's behaving with humility, modesty and the fear of sin to the greatest possible degree. One should also to the utmost degree, remain at a distance from pride, anger, fussiness, foolishness and evil gossip. One should abstain from idle conversation and flying off the handle, even with members of one's own household.

2. Melancholia is, by itself, an exceedingly unpleasant personal quality, especially for people whose intention is to acquire esoteric knowledge and experience the Holy Spirit. Nothing impedes mystical inspiration—even for someone who is otherwise worthy of it—more than the quality of sadness.

3. Additionally, the quality of anger, aside from serving as an obstacle to mystical inspiration altogether [has other injurious repercussions]. My teacher, of blessed memory [the Ari] used to be more exacting when it came to anger than with all other transgressions, even in a situation where a person explodes in anger for the sake of some religious obligation. This is because all other transgressions injure only a single limb of the body, whereas the quality of anger injures the soul in its entirety, altering the character completely. This is the issue: when we lose our temper, the holy soul departs from us altogether. In its place there enters a soul of an evil nature. This is the esoteric meaning of the verse from Job (18:4) "You who tear yourself in your anger." Such a person actually tears the holy soul, rendering it unfit at the moment of wrath.

Acknowledgment

(To be said while standing in the synagogue of the Ari or at his grave in the cemetery just below.)

For the sake of the unification of the Holy One Blessed be He and his Sh'khinah, *behold I perform*

*the mitzvah of visiting Israel, in fear and love, love
and fear, through the hidden and concealed One, in
the name of all Israel, and in order to give satisfac-
tion to my creator and maker, and in order to raise
the Sh'khinah from the dust.*

בָּרוּךְ אַתָּה יְיָ אֱלֹהֵינוּ מֶלֶךְ הָעוֹלָם גּוֹאֵל יִשְׂרָאֵל.

*Barukh atah Adonai Eloheinu melekh ha'olam,
go'el yisra'el.*

Blessed is God, redeemer of Israel.[8]

Afterthoughts

This Place Is Holy

God said to Abram, "Raise your eyes
and look out from where you are,
tsafonah v'negbah v'kedmah v'yamah,
to the north and south, to the east and west,
for I give all the land that you see
to you and your ancestors forever."
—*Genesis 13:14–15*

THE NEGEV:
"Negbah—to the South"

Dead Sea and Sodom

The outrage of Sodom and Gomorrah is so great
and their sin so grave. . . .

—*Genesis 18:20*

Anticipation

This is Israel's "Death Valley," a descent from the craggy
mountains to sea level and then beyond, reaching the lowest
point in the earth's surface! Metaphorically too, it is the low
point of human existence, the location of Sodom and Gomorrah, cities so sinful that they had to be destroyed from
the face of the earth. The Bible leaves little doubt about the
horrors that transpired here: rampant violence, sexual abuse
and licentiousness were common public practice. Abraham's
entreaty to save the town was insufficient because God
could not find even five good people there. In the end, angels dressed like men were sent to destroy it.

> As dawn broke, the angels urged Lot [Abraham's
> nephew] saying, "Up, take your wife and your two
> remaining daughters, lest you be swept away by
> the iniquity of the city." Still, he delayed. So the
> men seized his hand and the hands of his wife and
> his two daughters—in the Lord's mercy on him—
> and brought him out and left him outside the city.
> When they brought him outside, one of them said,
> "Flee for your life. Do not look behind you, nor
> stop anywhere along the Plain; flee to the hills. Lest
> you be swept away."
>
> The Lord rained upon Sodom and Gomorrah
> sulfurous fire from heaven. He annihilated those
> cities and the entire Plain. And all the inhabitants
> of the cities and the vegetation of the ground. Lot's
> wife, behind him, looked back, and she was there-
> upon turned into a pillar of salt (Genesis 19:15-17,
> 24–26).

The Dead Sea still bears her "name," in Hebrew—*Yam Hamelakh,* "The Salt Sea."

Approach

I've often wondered what Lot's wife saw,
Why she lost her soul for salt,
And now lies strewn around the water's edge, I
    guess,
part of its name, "The Salt Sea."
Was it wistfulness for her past,
Some secret urge to perpetuate the violence
At a distance,
At least to watch the city die
Like Mme. LaFarge who used to knit a stitch of
    pleasure
Each time the guillotine came slicing down.

The waters thick with salt and iodine and potash
And untold minerals fresh from some old chemistry
    textbook
Even smell like evil.
They boil up like tar in the hot desert sun.
Experience-starved tourists unload from buses to
    float in them,
Then shower endlessly to purge their skin
Of what the waters know deep down,
Of ancient human baseness.

I am no Mrs. Lot, but nonetheless, like her,
I cannot resist a backward glance at history here,
And I wonder . . .
Why have the Salt Sea's waters eroded so in recent
    years
(It's really just a puddle now compared to what it
    was)?
Could it be that when the Messiah comes
These waters thick with Sodom-memories will all
    dry up?

Acknowledgment

(To be said while looking out at the Dead Sea from its shores.)

עַל חֵטְא שֶׁחָטָאנוּ לְפָנֶיךָ
סְלַח לָנוּ מְחַל לָנוּ כַּפֶּר לָנוּ.

Al chet shechatanu l'fanekha,
s'lakh lanu, m'chal lanu, kaper lanu.

For the sins that we, the human race, have committed before You, God, forgive us, pardon us, grant us atonement.[9]

Afterthoughts

Ein Gedi

Streams come out of the rock,
waters flow down like rivers.

—Psalm 78:16

Anticipation

Nothing heralds hope more than an oasis in the wilderness. Appropriately, then, not far from the Dead Sea where nothing grows, and with the memory of Sodom's bestiality still somehow lying heavily in the hot desert air, there is a sign of hope: the oasis of Ein Gedi. Already in the Stone Age, some 6,000 years ago, our ancestors were coming here for the abundant water and lush vegetation. King Saul came here hunting for David, whom he suspected of treason. When, to Saul's surprise, David spared Saul's life, after coming across him unarmed and vulnerable to attack, Saul proclaimed David's succession to the throne.

Ein Gedi is a place where it is easy to believe in a messianic coming. You climb away from desert waste and come to waterfalls that splash happily on picnickers who seem to have left all cares back in the desert sand. All around are shrubs and trees and cacti, practically inviting you to take their picture in the shininess of the midday sun.

If the sins of Sodom represent an image of inhumanity and its neighboring Dead Sea the epitome of death, Ein Gedi presents the positive pole of love and life. Its theme was recognized early in the Bible itself, when the anonymous author of the Song of Songs described Ein Gedi as the place best suited for making love.

Take the time to climb through Ein Gedi's paths up and out of the desert heat; let its cool clear water wash away all anxiety. Dream of the messianic promise of King David, and the sheer joy of love—life at its oasis best.

Approach

The Song of Songs, 1:2–8, 12–14[10]

יִשָּׁקֵנִי מִנְּשִׁיקוֹת פִּיהוּ
כִּי טוֹבִים דֹּדֶיךָ מִיָּיִן:
לְרֵיחַ שְׁמָנֶיךָ טוֹבִים
שֶׁמֶן תּוּרַק שְׁמֶךָ
עַל כֵּן עֲלָמוֹת אֲהֵבוּךָ:

מָשְׁכֵנִי אַחֲרֶיךָ נָּרוּצָה
הֱבִיאַנִי הַמֶּלֶךְ חֲדָרָיו
נָגִילָה וְנִשְׂמְחָה בָּךְ
נַזְכִּירָה דֹדֶיךָ מִיַּיִן
מֵישָׁרִים אֲהֵבוּךָ:

שְׁחוֹרָה אֲנִי וְנָאוָה
בְּנוֹת יְרוּשָׁלָיִם
כְּאָהֳלֵי קֵדָר
כִּירִיעוֹת שְׁלֹמֹה:
אַל תִּרְאֻנִי
שֶׁאֲנִי שְׁחַרְחֹרֶת
שֶׁשְּׁזָפַתְנִי הַשָּׁמֶשׁ:

הַגִּידָה לִּי שֶׁאָהֲבָה נַפְשִׁי
אֵיכָה תִרְעֶה
אֵיכָה תַּרְבִּיץ בַּצָּהֳרָיִם
שַׁלָּמָה אֶהְיֶה כְּעֹטְיָה
עַל עֶדְרֵי חֲבֵרֶיךָ:

אִם לֹא תֵדְעִי לָךְ הַיָּפָה בַּנָּשִׁים
צְאִי לָךְ בְּעִקְבֵי הַצֹּאן
וּרְעִי אֶת גְּדִיֹּתַיִךְ
עַל מִשְׁכְּנוֹת הָרֹעִים:

עַד שֶׁהַמֶּלֶךְ בִּמְסִבּוֹ
נִרְדִּי נָתַן רֵיחוֹ:
צְרוֹר הַמֹּר דּוֹדִי לִי
בֵּין שָׁדַי יָלִין:
אֶשְׁכֹּל הַכֹּפֶר דּוֹדִי לִי
בְּכַרְמֵי עֵין גֶּדִי:

I long for his kiss; the kisses of his mouth!
Your love is better than wine.
Your anointing oil is fragrant,
Your name is perfume poured out.
No wonder the girls love you!

Take me along, quickly,
A king who admits me to his bedroom.
We will rejoice on your account,
Extol your love—better than wine.
For good reason they do love you!

I am black and beautiful,
O women of Jerusalem,
Like the tents of Kedar,
and the curtains of Solomon.
Will you stare at me with your eyes
Because I am dark
Because the sun has looked me through?

Tell me, O my deepest love,
Where you pasture your flock,
Where you lie them down at noon-time.
Why should I play hide-and-seek
Among the flocks of your friends?

If you do not know, most beautiful woman,
Follow the tracks of the flock
And pasture your kids
Where the shepherds lie. . . .

Before the king arrives at his couch,
My perfume hovered fragrantly.
My love will lie between my breasts.
Like a sack of myrrh,
A cluster of blossoms,
Picked from the vineyards of Ein Gedi.

Acknowledgment

(To be recited, if possible, at one of the waterfalls, preferably the highest one, where water cascades down into a pool of water.)

Psalm 65:9–13

וַיִּירְאוּ יֹשְׁבֵי קְצָוֹת מֵאוֹתֹתֶיךָ
מוֹצָאֵי בֹקֶר וָעֶרֶב תַּרְנִין:
פָּקַדְתָּ הָאָרֶץ וַתְּשֹׁקְקֶהָ
רַבַּת תַּעְשְׁרֶנָּה
פֶּלֶג אֱלֹהִים מָלֵא מָיִם
תָּכִין דְּגָנָם כִּי כֵן תְּכִינֶהָ:
תְּלָמֶיהָ רַוֵּה נַחֵת גְּדוּדֶיהָ
בִּרְבִיבִים תְּמֹגְגֶנָּה
צִמְחָהּ תְּבָרֵךְ:
עִטַּרְתָּ שְׁנַת טוֹבָתֶךָ
וּמַעְגָּלֶיךָ יִרְעֲפוּן דָּשֶׁן:
יִרְעֲפוּ נְאוֹת מִדְבָּר
וְגִיל גְּבָעוֹת תַּחְגֹּרְנָה:

You visit the earth and water it,
You greatly enrich it.
The river of God is full of water;
You provide the people with grain,
For so You have prepared it.
You water its furrows abundantly,
Settling its ridges,
Softening it with showers,
And blessing its growth.
You crown the year with your bounty,
Your wagon tracks overflow with richness.
The pastures of the wilderness overflow.
The hills gird themselves with joy.
The meadows clothe themselves with flocks.
The valleys deck themselves with grain.
They shout and sing together for joy.

בָּרוּךְ אַתָּה יְיָ אֱלֹהֵינוּ מֶלֶךְ הָעוֹלָם מְבָרֵךְ הַשָּׁנִים.

Barukh atah Adonai Eloheinu melekh ha'olam,
m'varekh hashanim.

Blessed is God, for blessing our years.[11]

Afterthoughts

At a Kibbutz in the Negev

Clear a road in the desert for Adonai.
Level a highway in the wilderness for our God.

—Isaiah 40:3

Anticipation

Tragedy is a soul without a body, and comedy, a
body without a soul. King Lear in the forest, who
used to have a body: throne, followers, scepter, a red
robe on his shoulders and a crown on his head, and
lost that body—he is tragic. And on the other hand,
when the clown comes on stage and puts on a body
royal, but inside, remains what he was—this is comedy. So far we have been tragedy, an abstract soul
without a body. And the state—this is the form, the
body we put on.

So spoke David Ben-Gurion, who spoke also for others of his generation who understood the need for a Jewish
"body": ordinary men and women who would work the
ground, develop industry, vote for a government, and walk
the streets of cities and of towns, free and unafraid.

So much of Israel is now so built up that it is hard to
recognize what a miracle it all once was. It is hard to believe
that there once were swamps in the Galil, that Tel Aviv was
only sand dunes, or that Jerusalem was a dusty colonial out-
post ravaged by filth and disease.

But the desert still speaks of a miracle in the making.
Stand just a mile or two outside the settlements and you understand immediately why everyone said, "You cannot settle
people in the Negev." But we did. And we still are. The bulk
of the land is still what it has been for centuries: unwatered
wasteland, pure wilderness where sandstorms rage, where no
water falls, and where the best you can expect is a *chamsin*,
a wind so saturated with heat it blows the desert dryness all

the way to Jerusalem and Tel Aviv. But here and there, the settlements stand out, magnets of opportunity for those still bold enough to pioneer a future.

Approach

Psalm 126

שִׁיר הַמַּעֲלוֹת,
בְּשׁוּב יְיָ אֶת שִׁיבַת צִיּוֹן
הָיִינוּ כְּחֹלְמִים.
אָז יִמָּלֵא שְׂחוֹק פִּינוּ
וּלְשׁוֹנֵנוּ רִנָּה,
אָז יֹאמְרוּ בַגּוֹיִם
הִגְדִּיל יְיָ לַעֲשׂוֹת עִם אֵלֶּה.
הִגְדִּיל יְיָ לַעֲשׂוֹת עִמָּנוּ
הָיִינוּ שְׂמֵחִים.

A song of ascents . . .
When our God brought back those who returned to
  Zion,
We were like dreamers.
Our mouth was filled with laughter
Our tongues with shouts of joy.
Among the nations, people said,
"Adonai has done great things for these people."
Adonai has done great things with us,
and we rejoice.

Restore our fortunes, O God,
Like the watercourses of the Negev.
May those who sow in tears
Reap with shouts of joy. . . .
Bringing in their sheaves.

(If you have an opportunity to eat at the kibbutz, see special prayers for the occasion, p. 215.)

Acknowledgment

(To be said in the fields of the kibbutz, looking out toward the desert round about it.)

Psalm 107:35–37

יָשֵׂם מִדְבָּר לַאֲגַם מַיִם
וְאֶרֶץ צִיָּה לְמֹצָאֵי מָיִם:
וַיּוֹשֶׁב שָׁם רְעֵבִים
וַיְכוֹנְנוּ עִיר מוֹשָׁב:
וַיִּזְרְעוּ שָׂדוֹת וַיִּטְּעוּ כְרָמִים וַיַּעֲשׂוּ פְּרִי תְבוּאָה:

God turns the desert into pools of water,
The parched land into springs of water.
And there, God lets the hungry live;
They establish a town to live in.
They sow fields, plant vineyards, and get a fruitful
*   field.*

בָּרוּךְ אַתָּה יְיָ אֱלֹהֵינוּ מֶלֶךְ הָעוֹלָם קוֹרֵא בַּמִּדְבָּר.

Barukh atah Adonai Eloheinu melekh ha'olam,
korei bamidbar.

Blessed is God, who calls out in the desert.[12]

Afterthoughts

Sedeh Boker—
David Ben-Gurion's Home

I will again set up the fallen booth of David . . .
I will restore my people Israel.

—*Amos 9:11, 14*

The Jewish nation is going through a revolution.
We shall not return to what we were.

—*David Ben-Gurion*

Anticipation

"You cannot buy a commonwealth; you cannot conquer a commonwealth. You have to create it by your own work. We don't want to say that this is our country because we conquered it, but because we made it, we remade it, we created it." So argued David Ben-Gurion, in a speech that he described as his most representative address, his finest hour. It was delivered in 1946 as an impassioned appeal to the Anglo-American Committee that threatened to keep even survivors of Hitler's camps out of Israel.

It might equally have served as Ben-Gurion's own epitaph, since no one more than he "made" the State of Israel, then frequently "remade it," and finally "created it" into the democratic republic we know today.

Born in Russia in 1886, he eventually settled in the Negev, a fitting place for a man who epitomized toughness, vision and endurance. It was Ben-Gurion who insisted on declaring the State of Israel immediately upon the termination of the British mandate. It was he who became the first prime minister; who directed the War of Independence; who declared Jerusalem to be Israel's capital. It was he who demanded and exemplified the Jewish state when most of the world opposed it, and many less courageous Jewish souls were afraid to risk it.

To visit his home in the heart of the Negev is to return to a time when the ovens of Auschwitz had barely cooled, the world's powers jockeyed for their own advantage, and this single-minded leader acted on a promise he had made to a conference of Jewish survivors at Bergen–Belsen, "We shall not rest until every one of you who so desires joins us in the land of Israel to build a Jewish state."

Approach

David Ben-Gurion: Statement to the Anglo-American Committee, 1946

I realize the intellectual difficulty of our case. There is no precedent for the history of the Jewish People and there is no parallel to the fate of this country, no precedent for the special significance this country has for us. There is no parallel to the relations between our People and this country. It is unique. People usually think in analogies and when they are faced with a new phenomenon, they prefer to deny the existence of what they do not understand. But it remains a fact, nevertheless. You have the unique case of the homeless Jewish People and their historic country.

One reason why Jews came over here is love of Zion, a deep passionate love, strong as death. There is no parallel to that in all of human history. It is unique but it is a fact. You will see it here. There are 600,000 of us here because of that deep undying love of Zion.

What is the source of this love? A man may change many things, even his religion, even his wife, even his name. There is one thing which a man cannot change, his parents. The parents of our People are this country. It is unique, but there it is.

More than 300 years ago, a ship by the name of the *Mayflower* left Plymouth for the New World. It was a great event in American and English history. I wonder how many people know exactly the date when that ship left Plymouth, how many people were on that ship, and what kind of bread those people ate when they left Plymouth.

Well, more than 3,300 years ago, the Jews left Egypt. It was more than 3,000 years before the *Mayflower*, and every Jew in the world knows exactly the date when we left. It was on the fifteenth day of Nisan. The bread they ate was *matzah*. Up to this very day, all the Jews in the world on the fifteenth day of Nisan eat the same *matzah* and tell the story of the exile in Egypt. They tell what happened, and finish with these two sentences: "This year we were slaves; next year we shall be free. This year we are here; next year we shall be in the Land of Israel."[13]

Acknowledgment

בָּרוּךְ אַתָּה יְיָ אֱלֹהֵי דָוִד.

Barukh atah Adonai, Elohei david.

Blessed is God, the God of David.[14]

Afterthoughts

Masada

Anticipation

All the world now knows about Masada, the mighty fortress
in the Judean desert outfitted by King Herod between the
years 37 and 31 B.C.E. as his palace; then the site of the last
resistance and ultimate suicide of the Zealots, who had fled
the Jerusalem siege by Rome in 73 C.E. It reached symbolic prominence in a poem by Yitzchak Lamdan, published
in 1927. He spoke for the generation of pioneers risking
self-sacrifice in their homeland rather than replicate endlessly the plight of defenseless Jews in eastern Europe. The
hero of the poem is a pioneer who affirms, "I was sent by
my people and will endure any hardship for them. The God
of Masada is 'the God of the brave few.'"

By the 1960s, Masada was fully excavated, and immediately captured the Jewish imagination despite the trou-
bling theme of the Jews who committed suicide rather than
face capture by the Romans. Year after year, recruits to the
armed forces climbed its snake path as the final leg of a desert march that lasted two days and two nights. After changing clothes, they would regroup in formal parade formation
for a torchlight swearing-in ceremony during which each
recruit would receive a weapon and a Bible.

On December 15, 1986, the swearing-in ceremony
atop Masada was abandoned. Its underlying message of heroes who commit suicide no longer captured the imagination of a Jewish state which emphasized life, not death, and
victory rather than defeat. But the ideal of military self-suf-
ficiency and the need to remain firm in the commitment
to Israel's defense remains as much a part of Israeli culture
as ever.

Approach

The speech by Eliezer, leader at Masada.
From *Wars of the Jews*, Flavius Josephus

Since we, long ago, my generous friends, resolved never to be servants to the Romans, nor to give obedience to any other than God, who alone is the true and just master of humanity, the time has come obliging us to make that resolution true in practice. Let us not at this time bring a reproach upon ourselves for self-contradiction. If formerly we would not undergo slavery, must we now choose such intolerable punishments? This will occur if the Romans take power over us while we still live. We were the very first to revolt against them.

I cannot but deem it a favor that God has granted us, that we still have the power to die bravely and in a state of freedom—which has not been the case with others who were conquered unexpectedly. It is very plain that we shall be taken within a day's time; but it is still possible to die gloriously together with our dearest friends. This is what our enemies themselves cannot by any means prevent, although they want to take us alive. We simply cannot still propose that we fight them off and beat them.

To be sure, we dimly hoped to preserve ourselves still in a state of freedom, as we had been guilty of no sins ourselves against God, nor been partner to the sins of others. We also taught others to preserve their liberty. But consider how God has convinced us that our hopes were in vain, by bringing upon us the distress of the desperate state in which we now find ourselves. It is beyond anything we might have anticipated, since the nature of this fortress, in itself unconquerable, has not proved a means for our deliverance. Even though we still have food in great abundance and a vast quantity (more than we want) of arms and other necessities, we are openly deprived by God of all hope of deliverance.

This was the result of God's anger against us for our many sins of which we are guilty in a most extravagant and insolent way, with regard to our fellow citizens; the punishment for which let us not receive from the Romans, but from God, as executed by our own hands, for the latter will be more moderate than the former. Let our wives die be-fore they are raped, and our children before they have tasted slavery; and after we have slain them, let us bestow that glorious benefit upon one another mutually, and preserve ourselves in freedom, as an excellent funeral memorial to ourselves.

But first, let us destroy our money and the for-tress, by fire, for I am well assured that the Romans will be greatly saddened to find themselves unable to seize our bodies and our wealth as well. Let us spare nothing but our provisions, for they will be a testimonial when we are dead that we were not subdued for want of necessities, but that, in keep-ing with our original resolution, we have preferred death to slavery.

Acknowledgment

(To be said, perhaps, in the synagogue atop Masada.)

בְּיָדוֹ אַפְקִיד רוּחִי, בְּעֵת אִישַׁן וְאָעִירָה.
וְעִם רוּחִי גְּוִיָּתִי, יְיָ לִי וְלֹא אִירָא.
בָּרוּךְ אַתָּה יְיָ אֱלֹהֵינוּ מֶלֶךְ הָעוֹלָם
שׁוֹמֵר עַמּוֹ יִשְׂרָאֵל לָעַד.

B'yado afkid ruchi b'eit ishan v'a'ira,
V'im ruchi g'viyati; Adonai li v'lo ira
Barukh atah Adonai Eloheinu melekh ha'olam,
*   shomer amo yisra'el la'ad*

I place my soul in God's care when I sleep and
    when I wake.
And with my soul, my body; God is with me; I do
    not fear.
Blessed is God who guards our people Israel for-
    ever.[15]

Afterthoughts

JERUSALEM AND VICINITY:
"*Kedmah*—to the East"

Allenby Bridge

It may be your destiny to be a bridge between Asia and Europe. That, I firmly believe, is the mission of Zionism.

—*Sir Mark Sykes of the British Foreign Office,*
addressing a mass meeting at the London Opera House
following the Balfour Declaration

Anticipation

On October 31, 1917, Lord Balfour announced Great Britain's intention to establish a Jewish state. London's *Jewish Chronicle* waxed eloquent over England, "The friend of our people for generations. . . . Never was she truer to her noble traditions than today—never more England than now!"

On December 2 British Jews gathered to celebrate Balfour's declaration. The eminent Lord Rothschild presided and handed the microphone to Herbert Samuel, the cabinet member who had jockeyed for the bill behind the scenes, and who now, for the first time, gave public expression to the arguments behind the Zionist dream. He concluded his remarks with the final line from the Haggadah, *L'shanah haba'ah birushalayim*, "Next year in Jerusalem." Chief Rabbi Hertz recited Psalm 126, "When our God brought back those who returned to Zion, we were like dreamers," and reminded the people that many centuries ago, another set of exiles (living in Babylonia) had gone home. Rabbi Moses Gaster, a scholar and leader of the British Sefardi community, followed, recalling an old legend that when the Temple fell, bits of its masonry lodged in the heart of every Jew. Gaster concluded, "I feel the stone in my heart already loosening."

Jews throughout the world waited anxiously to see if Britain would make good on its promise. Then, one day, their attention was drawn to a tiny bridge named for General Edmund Allenby, no Zionist sympathizer himself, but a loyal soldier at war with Turkey, and anxious to build a base of operations in Palestine. His troops attacked Jerusalem from the east on November 18, and less than a month later, Jerusalem was in British hands. On December 11, Allenby (accompanied by General T.E. Lawrence, better known as Lawrence of Arabia) entered the city.

"It was a brilliant day," Allenby wrote home to his wife. "Hoar frost here, in the early A.M., and then iced sunshine, with no wind. We could see, from the top of the house, the mountains of Moab; deep blue and huge. The Dead Sea lay too low to be seen."

Allenby rode through the area outside the Old City's walls, and then dismounted to enter the Jaffa gate on foot, the first Christian to capture the city since the Crusaders. Muslim soldiers from India were already guarding the Dome of the Rock, and Jewish units would arrive in less than three months. It was, he said, "the supreme moment of the war."[16]

Approach

Declaration of General Allenby,
December 11, 1917

To the inhabitants of Jerusalem the Blessed and to the people dwelling in the vicinity:

The defeat inflicted upon the troops of the Turks by the troops under my command has resulted in the occupation of your city by my forces. I therefore, here and now, declare it to be under martial law. . . .

Since your city is regarded with affection by the adherents of three of the great religions of mankind, and its soil has been consecrated by the prayers and pilgrimages of devout people of those three religions for many centuries, therefore do I make known to you that every sacred building, monument, holy spot, shrine, traditional site, endowment, pious bequest, or customary place of prayer, of whatsoever form of the three religions, will be maintained and protected according to the existing customs and beliefs of those to whose faith they are sacred.

Acknowledgment

(To be recited after crossing the border into or out of Jordan, at the first available opportunity.)

כָּל הָעוֹלָם כֻּלּוֹ גֶּשֶׁר צַר מְאֹד.

Kol ha'olam kulo gesher tsar m'od.

The whole world is a narrow bridge.

מִן הַמֵּצַר קָרָאתִי יָהּ
עָנָנִי בַמֶּרְחַבְיָהּ

*Min hameitsar karati Yah
Anani vamerchavyah*

In a narrow place, I called to God.
God answered me with great expansiveness.

שִׁיר הַמַּעֲלוֹת,
בְּשׁוּב יְיָ אֶת שִׁיבַת צִיּוֹן
הָיִינוּ כְּחֹלְמִים.
אָז יִמָּלֵא שְׂחוֹק פִּינוּ
וּלְשׁוֹנֵנוּ רִנָּה,
אָז יֹאמְרוּ בַגּוֹיִם
הִגְדִּיל יְיָ לַעֲשׂוֹת עִם אֵלֶּה.
הִגְדִּיל יְיָ לַעֲשׂוֹת עִמָּנוּ
הָיִינוּ שְׂמֵחִים.

*Shir hama'alot
B'shuv Adonai et shivat tsiyon
hayinu k'cholmim
Az yimalei s'chok pinu
Ul'shoneinu rinah
Az yomru vagoyim
Higdil Adonai la'asot im eleh
Higdil Adonai la'asot imanu
Hayinu s'meikhim*

A song of ascents . . .
When our God brought back those who returned
   to Zion,

We were like dreamers.
Our mouth was filled with laughter
Our tongues with shouts of joy.
Among the nations, people said,
"Adonai has done great things for these people."
Adonai has done great things with us,
and we rejoice.[17]

בָּרוּךְ אַתָּה יְיָ אֱלֹהֵינוּ מֶלֶךְ הָעוֹלָם הָעֹנֶה בְּיוֹם צָרֵנוּ.

Barukh atah Adonai Eloheinu melekh ha'olam,
ha'oneh b'yom tsareinu.

Blessed is God, who answers in times of trouble.

Afterthoughts

At the Jaffa Gate

Adonai loves the gates of Zion.

—Psalm 87:2

Anticipation

There is something about a gate. Jacob thought the angels in his dream came from "The Gate of Heaven." Yom Kippur's final service is called *N'illah*, the "closing of the gates," in this case, the gates of the ancient temple that clanged shut when the service ended. Judaism imagines human life as a series of gates opening and closing, opportunities gained and lost, chapters of our biography begun or ended. Fittingly, Jerusalem is best known as a city with seven gates. Nothing can sufficiently prepare you for your entry into the Old City's gates, probably the Jaffa Gate, the gate through which most people first enter the city. For your Approach tomorrow we provide a poetic translation of Naomi Shemer's magnificent song *Y'rushalayim Shel Zahav*, and suggest that the night before entering the Old City, your group gather to sing it together. If you are alone, be sure to read it before you go to sleep.

All but the last stanza of the song was composed before 1967, when the old city was still in Jordanian hands. It reflected the barrenness of the Old City, bereft of a Jewish presence, and the blockade that prevented Jews from heading south around the city into the area of the Dead Sea, Jericho, and Hebron. But that very year, Jerusalem fell into Israeli hands, and was reopened for Jewish pilgrimage and settlement. A fourth and final verse was added to reflect the new situation and celebrate our return.

When you get to the Jaffa Gate, pause long enough to make a complete three-hundred-and-sixty-degree turn in the street, letting your eye take in as far as it can see in the space between the wall of the Old City and the new buildings that have gone up everywhere outside of it. Imagine what it was like when Jordanian guns, mounted on the Old City's walls, rained fire down into the abandoned square where you now stand. This place, which was a "no-man's land" separated on both sides by barbed wire, is now Jerusalem's dominant portal to its past, a place where everyone may enter in peace.

Approach

No poem better records the transformation of the divided city into a unified Jerusalem, with the Old City its spiritual center. If you are traveling in a group, take the time to gather outside the gate or in your hotel before leaving to sing it together.

יְרוּשָׁלַיִם שֶׁל זָהָב,
וְשֶׁל נְחֹשֶׁת וְשֶׁל אוֹר,
הֲלֹא לְכָל שִׁירַיִךְ
אֲנִי כִּנּוֹר!

Y'rushalayim shel zahav,
V'shel n'choshet v'shel or,
Halo l'khol shirayikh
Ani kinor

Y'rushalayim, built of gold,
Built of copper, built of light,
For your songs, I'm a fiddler,
By day and by night

The fragrance of the scented pine trees,
The wine-clear mountain air,
Form winds that greet the nearing evening
To sounds of bells everywhere.
In trees and stones asleep, aslumber,
A captive of its dreams,
The Temple sits inside our city,
Alone and unredeemed.

Y'rushalayim . . .

The ancient cisterns without water,
An empty city square,
The Temple mount without its keepers,
A city lone and bare.
And through the rocks and through the caverns,
The winds of sorrow roar.
The path by Jericho's untread now,
Down to the Dead Sea shore.

Y'rushalayim . . .

Yet still today I sing your beauty,
Place crowns upon your walls,
I'm younger than your youngest child,
A poet meek and small.
But your name—a kiss of angels—
Burns fiery and bold.
I'll not forget *Y'rushalayim*,
Our city built of gold.

Y'rushalayim . . .

To ancient cisterns, to the city,
We have come back again.
From the Temple Mount the shofar heralds,
The name, "Jerusalem."
And through the rocks and through the caverns,
There shine a thousand suns.
The path by Jericho announces
Our journey's just begun.

Acknowledgment

To be recited immediately after walking through the gate.

Psalm 122

שִׁיר הַמַּעֲלוֹת: לְדָוִד.
שָׂמַחְתִּי בְּאֹמְרִים לִי
בֵּית יְיָ נֵלֵךְ.

עֹמְדוֹת הָיוּ רַגְלֵינוּ
בִּשְׁעָרַיִךְ, יְרוּשָׁלָיִם
יְרוּשָׁלַיִם, הַבְּנוּיָה
כְּעִיר שֶׁחֻבְּרָה לָּהּ יַחְדָּו
שֶׁשָּׁם עָלוּ שְׁבָטִים
שִׁבְטֵי יָהּ עֵדוּת לְיִשְׂרָאֵל,
לְהוֹדוֹת לְשֵׁם יְיָ.
כִּי שָׁמָּה יָשְׁבוּ כִסְאוֹת לְמִשְׁפָּט,
כִּסְאוֹת לְבֵית דָּוִיד.
שַׁאֲלוּ שְׁלוֹם יְרוּשָׁלָיִם
יִשְׁלָיוּ אֹהֲבָיִךְ.
יְהִי שָׁלוֹם בְּחֵילֵךְ,
שַׁלְוָה בְּאַרְמְנוֹתָיִךְ.
לְמַעַן אַחַי וְרֵעָי,
אֲדַבְּרָה נָּא שָׁלוֹם בָּךְ.
לְמַעַן בֵּית יְיָ אֱלֹהֵינוּ
אֲבַקְשָׁה טוֹב לָךְ.

I rejoiced when they said to me,
"Let us go to the house of Adonai."
Here we stand within your gates,
O Jerusalem . . .

Pray for the peace of Jerusalem.
May they who love you prosper.
Peace be within your walls,
And security within your towers.
For the sake of family and friends,
I will now say, "Peace be within you."
For the sake of the house of Adonai our God,
I will seek your good.

בָּרוּךְ אַתָּה יְיָ אֱלֹהֵינוּ מֶלֶךְ הָעוֹלָם
הַמַּחֲזִיר שְׁכִינָתוֹ לְצִיּוֹן

Barukh atah Adonai Eloheinu melekh ha'olam,
hamachazir sh'khinato l'tsiyon.

Blessed is God, present again in Zion.[18]

Afterthoughts

In Old Jerusalem

Walk about Zion, go all around it, count its towers.
Consider well its ramparts, go through its citadels.
That you may tell the next generation,
"This is God."

—*Psalm 48:13–14*

Anticipation

There are many ancient cities, but there is only one ancient Jerusalem. When you walk its streets, you rub shoulders with your own family's history. As you quickly discover, you are a pilgrim in time, not just in space. The minute you enter from the Jaffa Gate, for instance, you see on your right remnants of the homes from the days of the Maccabees, while tunnels recently excavated under the eastern Temple Mount take you back to civilizations that flourished here long before King David was even born.

Just short of the Wall, there is the Jewish Quarter of today where settlers make new history while bustling past barely noticed ruins of medieval synagogues. To the nearby north, Christians walk the route called the *Via Dolorosa,* the path that Jesus took on his way to the cross. On the other side of the *Kotel* Muslims kneel in prayer at the Dome of the Rock, the mosque that honors the place where Mohammed is said to have been spirited to heaven.

We Jews take time travel well back before either of those events, obviously, but we stop to capture memories of less distant eras also; and we bring more history than we take away, for we each bring stories of our own, as A. M. Klein, the Jewish "poet laureate" from Canada wrote:

> I lift my visor. Know me who I am. . . .
> To those that begat me
> This body is residence. Corpuscular,
> They dwell in my veins, they eavesdrop at my ear,
> They circle, as with Torahs, round my skull,

In exit and in entrance all day long pull
The latches of my heart, descend, and rise—
And there look generations through my eyes.[19]

You want to walk Jerusalem's streets to capture the profound religious truth that "there look generations through
your eyes." Walk around the city walls perhaps; stop to see
what your great grandparents could only dream about from
far-off ghetto homes. Take back memories, but leave some
there as well—as poet Yehuda Amichai did, in the poem he
recited when first he entered old Jerusalem after the Six Day
War, finding spiritual echoes in even an old Arab's shop. You
will read his poem tomorrow, as you approach your Jerusalem walk through time.

Approach

On Yom Kippur, Yehuda Amichai

*On Yom Kippur in 1967, I put on my dark holi-
    day suit*
And went to the old city of Jerusalem.
*I stood for a long time before the alcove of an old
    Arab's shop,*
Not far from the gates of Shechem [Nablus], a shop
Of buttons and zippers and spools of thread
In every color; and of snaps and buckles.
A glorious light and a great many colors,
Like a holy ark with its doors ajar.

I told him in my heart that my father too
Had a shop of such threads and buttons.
*I explained to him in my heart about all the tens of
    years*
*And the reasons and the circumstances because of
    which I am now here*
*And my father's shop is in ashes there, and he is
    buried here.*

By the time I was finished, it was time for N'illah.
He too pulled down the shutter and locked the gate,
And I went back home with all the worshippers.

Acknowledgment

(To be said, perhaps, at one of the restored synagogues in the Old City.)

בָּרוּךְ יְיָ מִצִּיּוֹן
שֹׁכֵן יְרוּשָׁלָיִם.

Barukh Adonai mitsiyon,
shochen y'rushalayim.

From Zion, let God be blessed.
God who dwells in Jerusalem.[20]

Afterthoughts

Har Herzl

If you will it, it is no dream.

—Theodor Herzl (1860–1904)

Anticipation

Har Herzl, the mountain on which Herzl's grave now stands, holds also the resting place of Israel's many heroes, military and ideological. There is much to move you here: Herzl's grave itself, for instance, which symbolizes the dream for which all those buried here gave their lives; the memorial to Yitzchak Rabin, cut down in 1995 at a peace rally by an assassin intent on "holy" war. These two great men are bookends in time, both of them visionaries, one for landedness after centuries of Diaspora life, the other for peace when all he knew was chronic war.

Most people head directly to Rabin's grave but take the time to visit Herzl's tomb as well. Like Moses, who never actually set foot in the Promised Land, Herzl too died without seeing his dream come true. Though he envisioned modern Israel, he never saw it born.

The Torah records how Joseph came to Pharaoh after Jacob died, pleading, "My father made me swear, saying, 'I am about to die. Be sure to bury me in the grave which I made ready for myself in the Land of Canaan.' Now therefore, let me go up and bury my father" (Genesis 50:5). When Joseph himself lay dying, "He made the Israelites swear, saying, "When God has taken notice of you, carry my bones up from here'" (Genesis 50:25). God took notice of the Jewish People, and we brought Herzl's remains to rest here too. He therefore lies reburied in the center of what is truly one of the most peaceful and moving spots in all Jerusalem.

Approach

At Herzl's Grave

Opening entry in *The Complete Diaries*
of Theodor Herzl[21]

Paris, around Pentecost, 1895. For some time past, I have been occupied with a work of infinite grandeur. At the moment I do not know if I shall carry it through. It looks like a mighty dream. But for days and weeks, it has possessed me beyond the limits of consciousness. It accompanies me wherever I go, hovers behind my ordinary talk, looks over my shoulder at my comically trivial journalistic work, disturbs me and intoxicates me.

It is still too early to surmise what will come of it, but my experience tells me that even as a dream it is something remarkable, and that I ought to write it down—if not as a reminder to humanity, then at least for my own delight and reflection in later years. And perhaps as something between these two possibilities—that is, as literature. If my conception is not translated into reality, at least out of my activity can come a novel.

Title: The Promised Land!

.... How I proceeded from the idea of writing a novel to a practical program is already a mystery to me, although it happened within a few weeks. It is in the realm of the unconscious.

Perhaps these ideas are not practical ones at all, and I am only making a laughing-stock of myself to the people with whom I talk about it seriously. Could I be a figure in my own novel?

At Rabin's Grave

"We've known each other fifty years,"
said Shimon Peres of Yitzchak Rabin.
"He never agreed to sing."

But sing he did, a song of peace,
His final legacy,

"Our bitter cries will not revive
the man whose candle is snuffed out,
The woman buried in the earth.

But let the sun shine through the flowers.
Do not look backward.
Don't just whisper prayers.
Sing out boldly songs of peace."

Hear his intimations of a messianic age,
The budding hope of better times
Plucked unripened from a world still raw with rage,
But pregnant with the taste of peace.

Acknowledgment

(To be said while standing directly before these grave sites.)

אֵל מָלֵא רַחֲמִים,

שׁוֹכֵן בַּמְּרוֹמִים,

הַמְצֵא מְנוּחָה נְכוֹנָה

תַּחַת כַּנְפֵי הַשְּׁכִינָה,

בְּמַעֲלוֹת קְדוֹשִׁים וּטְהוֹרִים כְּזֹהַר הָרָקִיעַ מַזְהִירִים,

אֶת נִשְׁמוֹת כָּל אֵלֶּה שֶׁהָלְכוּ לְעוֹלָמָם

בְּגַן עֵדֶן תְּהֵא מְנוּחָתָם.

לָכֵן בַּעַל הָרַחֲמִים יַסְתִּירֵם בְּסֵתֶר כְּנָפָיו לְעוֹלָמִים,

וְיִצְרוֹר בִּצְרוֹר הַחַיִּים אֶת נִשְׁמוֹתֵיהֶם,

יְיָ הוּא נַחֲלָתָם,

וְיָנוּחוּ בְשָׁלוֹם עַל מִשְׁכְּבוֹתֵיהֶם,

וְנֹאמַר אָמֵן.

El malei rachamim

O God, full of compassion,
You who dwell on high,
Grant perfect rest beneath the shelter of your presence,
Among the holy and pure who shine like the
*   brightness of the skies,*
To those who gave their lives for our land and for
*   our people.*
May they repose in Paradise.
Bring them under the cover of your wings,
And let their souls be bound up in the bond of
*   eternal life.*
God, be their possession;
And let their repose be peaceful.
Amen.[22]

Afterthoughts

At the Knesset

In that day,
I will set up again the fallen booth of David;
I will restore my people Israel;
I will plant them upon their soil, never more to be uprooted.

—Amos 9:11, 14

Anticipation

Known most for its Chagall tapestries and its British-style raucous parliamentary proceedings, the Knesset yet has its spiritual and religious side. Physically, it dominates the landscape and displays the menorah which became Israel's symbolic link between old and new. Unlike the eight-branch variety used for Chanukah, this seven-branch sign of modern Israel was originally a fixture in the ancient Temple, regularly outfitted and lit by the *Kohanim*, the priests, of old. Traditional Jews avoid all three-dimensional copies of it, preferring to await the time when God rebuilds the ancient Temple with its original menorah intact. Seeing itself as a sacred center for modern Jews, the Jewish state replicated the ancient symbol as its official governmental image. Modern pilgrims can only imagine the thrill of receiving a letter from the British government in 1917, saying that Israel might some day be born; or standing near here in 1948, hearing the Declaration of Independence of the State of Israel being read. But at least we can imagine it by reading the historic letter from Britain's Lord Balfour, known ever after as the Balfour Declaration.

Foreign Office
November 2nd, 1917

Dear Lord Rothschild,
I have much pleasure in conveying to you, on behalf of His Majesty's Government, the following

declaration of sympathy with Jewish Zionist aspirations which has been submitted to and approved by the Cabinet.

"His Majesty's Government view with favour the establishment in Palestine of a national home for the Jewish people, and will use their best endeavours to facilitate the achievement of this object, it being clearly understood that nothing shall be done which may prejudice the civil and religious rights of existing non-Jewish communities in Palestine, or the rights and political status enjoyed by Jews in any other country."

I should be grateful if you would bring this declaration to the knowledge of the Zionist Federation.

Yours sincerely,
Arthur James Balfour

Approach

Declaration of the Establishment of the State of Israel[23]

Eretz Yisrael was the birthplace of the Jewish People. Here, their spiritual, religious and political identity was shaped. Here, they first attained to statehood, created cultural values of national and universal significance, and gave to the world the eternal Book of Books.

After being forcibly exiled from their land, the people kept faith with it throughout their dispersion and never ceased to pray and hope for their return to it, and for the restoration in it of their political freedom.

Impelled by this historic and traditional attachment, Jews strove in every successive generation to re-establish themselves in their ancient homeland. In recent decades they returned in their masses. Pioneers, *M'apilim*[24] and defenders, they made deserts bloom, revived the Hebrew language, built villages and towns, and created a thriving community, controlling its own economy and culture, loving peace but knowing how to defend itself, bringing the blessings of progress to all the country's inhabitants, and aspiring toward independent nationhood.

In the year 5657 (1897), at the summons of the spiritual father of the Jewish state, Theodor Herzl, the First Zionist Congress convened and proclaimed the right of the Jewish people to national rebirth in its own country.

The right was recognized in the Balfour Declaration of 2nd November, 1917, and reaffirmed in the mandate of the League of Nations, which, in particular, gave international sanction to the historic connection between the Jewish people and *Eretz Yisrael* and to the right of the Jewish people to rebuild its national home.

The catastrophe that recently befell the Jewish people—the massacre of millions of Jews in Europe—was another clear demonstration of the urgency of solving the problem of its homelessness by reestablishing in *Eretz Yisrael* the Jewish state which would open the gates of the homeland wide to every Jew and confer upon the Jewish people the state of a fully privileged member of the comity of nations.

Survivors of the Nazi Holocaust in Europe, as well as Jews from other parts of the world, continued to migrate to *Eretz Yisrael,* undaunted by difficulties, restrictions and dangers, and never ceased to assert their right to a life of dignity, freedom and honest toil in their national homeland.

In the Second World War, the Jewish community of this country contributed its full share to the struggle of the freedom- and peace-loving nations against the forces of the Nazi wickedness, and, by the blood of the soldiers and its war effort, gained the right to be reckoned among the peoples who founded the United Nations.

On the 29th November, 1947, The United Nations General Assembly passed a resolution calling for the establishment of a Jewish state in *Eretz Yisrael;* the General Assembly required the inhabitants of *Eretz Yisrael* to take such steps as were necessary on their part for the implementation of that resolution. This recognition by the United Nations of the right of the Jewish people to establish their state is irrevocable.

This right is the natural right of the Jewish people to be masters of their own fate, like all other nations, in their own sovereign state.

Accordingly, we, members of the People's Council representative of the Jewish community of *Eretz Yisrael* and of the Zionist Movement, are here assembled on the day of the termination of the British mandate over *Eretz Yisrael,* and, by virtue of our national and historic right, and on the strength of the resolution of the United Nations General Assembly, hereby declare the establishment of a Jewish state in *Eretz Yisrael,* to be known as the State of Israel.

We declare that, with effect from the moment of the termination of the Mandate, being tonight, the eve of the Sabbath, the 6th Iyar 5708 (15th May, 1948), until the establishment of the elected regular authorities of the State, in accordance with the constitution which shall be adopted by the elected Constituent Assembly, not later than the 1st October, 1948, the People's Council shall act as a provisional council of state, and its executive organ, the People's Administration, shall be the provisional government of the Jewish state to be called Israel.

The State of Israel will be open for Jewish immigration and for the ingathering of the exiles; it will foster the development of the country for the benefit of all inhabitants; it will be based on freedom, justice and peace as envisioned by the prophets of Israel; it will ensure complete equality of social and political rights to all inhabitants irrespective of religion, race or sex; it will guarantee freedom of religion, conscience, language, education and culture; it will safeguard the holy places of all religions; and it will be faithful to the principles of the charter of the United Nations.

The State of Israel is prepared to cooperate with the agencies and the representatives of the United Nations in implementing the resolution of the General Assembly of the 29th November 1947, and will take steps to implement the economic union of the whole of *Eretz Yisrael.*

We appeal to the United Nations to assist the Jewish people in the building-up of its State and to receive the State of Israel into the comity of nations.

We appeal—in the midst of the onslaught launched against us now for months—to the Arab inhabitants of the State of Israel to preserve peace and participate in the upbuilding of the State on the basis of full and equal citizenship and due representation in all the provisional institutions.

We extend our hand to all neighboring states and their peoples in an offer of peace and good neighborliness, and appeal to them to establish bonds of cooperation and mutual help with the sovereign Jewish people settled in its own land. The State of Israel is prepared to do its share in common effort for the advancement of the entire Middle East.

We appeal to the Jewish people throughout the Diaspora to rally round the Jews of *Eretz Yisrael* in the tasks of immigration and upbuilding and to stand by them in the great struggle for the realization of the age-old dream—the redemption of Israel.

Acknowledgment

(To be said, perhaps, in front of the Knesset, facing the large seven-branch menorah (candelabra) that is Israel's official state symbol.)

> *Avinu Shebashamayim:* Rock and Redeemer of the people Israel, bless the State of Israel, *reshit ts'michat ge'ulateinu,* the beginning of the dawn of our redemption. Shield it with your love; spread over it the shelter of your peace; send forth your light and truth to those who lead and judge it, and to those who hold elective office. Establish in them, through your presence, wise counsel, that they might walk in the way of justice, freedom and integrity. Strengthen the hands of those who guard our holy land. Let them inherit salvation and life. And give peace to the land, and perpetual joy to its inhabitants.

בָּרוּךְ אַתָּה יְיָ עֹשֶׂה שָׁלוֹם בִּמְרוֹמָיו
הוּא יַעֲשֶׂה שָׁלוֹם עָלֵינוּ וְעַל כָּל יִשְׂרָאֵל.

Barukh atah Adonai, oseh shalom bimromav hu ya'aseh shalom aleinu ve'al kol yisra'el.

Blessed is God, who makes peace on high, and will make peace on us and all of Israel.[25]

Afterthoughts

The Kotel *(The Wall)*

Know before whom you stand.

—*The Talmud*

Anticipation

The world is filled with walls that matter, some of them monumental in size or symbolism. The world's finances are still best symbolized by Wall Street, once a real wall at the north end of Manhattan's early population center. For centuries, the Great Wall of China defended Chinese from "barbarians." The Berlin Wall best represented the divided world of the Cold War, and its destruction, brick by brick, is probably the most fitting picture of the end of the Cold War.

For Jews, there is only one wall, *The* Wall, as it is called, or the *Kotel* in Hebrew. This is short for *Kotel Ma'aravi*, the Western Wall, because it stands at the western boundary of the Temple Mount, where it was once the retaining wall for the Temple's foundation. All that is left of the entire ancient Temple complex is this single simple structure. Jews have prayed here for centuries, wedging prayers scribbled onto paper into the crevices of its stones. If you have prayers with you from the people back home—or your own, for that matter—make sure you bring them with you.

Bring also your dreams and hopes. The Wall is a busy, noisy place, filled with Jews from all the world and Jews who live in its very shadows, all of whom are there in great numbers on any given day, saying their prayers. But it can be a private place too. Stake out a spot to touch it, even kiss it, if you dare. And just for a moment, be alone with God, and think the thoughts of Abraham Joshua Heschel who stood where you do and later wrote, "The Wall . . . . The old Mother crying for all of us. Stubborn, loving, waiting for redemption."[26]

Approach

(To be recited, perhaps, just outside the official area of the Wall, but in full view of it, ready to enter its precinct.)

From *Jerusalem, June 1967*
by Stanley F. Chyet

Who'd have dared shape the thought?
That we would come again to this antique rubble,
And that some definition of ourselves would grope
*   its way forth from these stones?*
That there was a backbone to the body of our mem-
*   ories,*
And that we could trace our backbone here,
In this eroded rock?
That millennia would not rob us of the longing to
*   stand here,*
Precisely here,
And that sophistications would not free us of the
*   need to exult here,*
Just here,
By this bone of Jerusalem,
With the great horn filling our ears?

Acknowledgment

(To be recited with one hand resting on the wall.)

The Wall is silent. For an instant, I am her tongue.
. . . O God, cleanse my lips, make me worthy to be
her tongue. [27]

(If you brought prayers from home, insert them into the crevices of the wall.)

Afterthoughts

The Temple Mount

In the days to come, the Holy One of Blessing
will hold a chorus for the righteous and will sit among them
in the Garden of Eden. They will point their fingers toward
Him, as it is said, "It will be said in that day: Behold, this is
our God for whom we waited that He might save us.
This is the Lord for whom we waited; we will be glad
and rejoice in His salvation (Isaiah 25:9)."

—*The Talmud (Ta'anit 31a)*

Anticipation

Above the *Kotel* is the actual plateau upon which the Temple
once stood. It is now home to the great Dome of the Rock
and the El Aqsa Mosque. This place's primal holiness cuts
through time and embodies the gulf of religious difference.

Controversy is not new here: not only between Jews
and Muslims, but among Jewish factions too. Strict Orthodox opinion forbids Jews from climbing the Temple Mount,
lest they unwittingly defile the place where sacrifices once
were offered. In fact, at the entrance to the pathway upward, you will find a warning sign and even a self-appointed
guardian announcing that Jews are forbidden to proceed.

Though contemporary Orthodox authorities are
rather unified on the matter, as late as one hundred years
ago, they were split on the issue. It actually goes back to a
twelfth-century debate between the famed Moses Maimonides and an outstanding critic of his, the Provencal authority
Abraham ben David. Maimonides held that the destruction of the Temple did not annul the sanctity of the spot on
which it stood. Ordinary Jews, therefore, should avoid standing in places reserved only for priests *(kohanim)*, and even
present-day *kohanim* should not appear there since, among
other things, they cannot dress in the required priestly dress,
the details of which we no longer even know. Jews who
are not Orthodox generally side with Abraham ben David,

who argued that the sanctity of the mount came to an end when the actual Temple and its altar were destroyed. They conclude that Jews may have access to the Temple Mount area as long as they respect the aura of the sacred that still hovers over it.

Approach

(From the pilgrim psalm, to be recited just before walking up the path to the Temple Mount.)

From Psalm 24

לְדָוִד מִזְמוֹר.
לַיהוה הָאָרֶץ וּמְלוֹאָהּ
תֵּבֵל וְיֹשְׁבֵי בָהּ.
כִּי הוּא עַל יַמִּים יְסָדָהּ
וְעַל נְהָרוֹת יְכוֹנְנֶהָ.
מִי יַעֲלֶה בְּהַר יהוה
וּמִי יָקוּם בִּמְקוֹם קָדְשׁוֹ?
נְקִי כַפַּיִם וּבַר לֵבָב
אֲשֶׁר לֹא נָשָׂא לַשָּׁוְא נַפְשִׁי
וְלֹא נִשְׁבַּע לְמִרְמָה.
יִשָּׂא בְרָכָה מֵאֵת יהוה
וּצְדָקָה מֵאֱלֹהֵי יִשְׁעוֹ.
זֶה דּוֹר דֹּרְשָׁיו
מְבַקְשֵׁי פָנֶיךָ יַעֲקֹב סֶלָה.

The earth is Adonai's and the fullness thereof,
The world and they that dwell therein.
For God founded it upon the seas,
and established it upon the floods.

Who shall ascend the mountain of God?
Who shall stand in God's holy place?
Those who have clean hands and a pure heart,
Who do not take God's name in vain,
And do not swear deceitfully.

They will receive blessing from Adonai,
And justice from the God of their salvation
Such is the company of those who seek our God,
Who seek to greet the God of Jacob.

Acknowledgment

(To be recited on the Temple Mount, close by the Dome of the Rock, which is said to be the place where the actual Temple sacrifice once took place.)

Our God and God of those who came before us:
May regard for us and memory of our ancestors rise
    before you,
With mindfulness of Jerusalem your holy city,
And heedfulness of your people, the House of Israel.
    for deliverance and for good,
    for grace, love, and mercy,
    for life and for peace
    On this day of our pilgrimage.

God remember us for good.
God visit us with blessing.
God save us for life.[28]

בָּרוּךְ אַתָּה יְיָ אֱלֹהֵינוּ מֶלֶךְ הָעוֹלָם
שֶׁאוֹתְךָ לְבַדְּךָ בְּיִרְאָה נַעֲבוֹד.

Barukh atah Adonai Eloheinu melekh ha'olam,
she'ot'kha l'vad'kha b'yir'ah na'avod.

Blessed is God, whom alone we serve in reverence.[29]

Afterthoughts

The Southern Wall
to the Temple Mount

"A song of ascents: Those who trust in our God are like
Mt. Zion, which cannot be moved, so abides eternally.
Our God blesses you out of Zion"

—*Psalms 125:1, 134:3*

Anticipation

You are about to retrace the steps taken by thousands of pilgrims when the Temple still stood. In an age without photographs, they would come from all over the Jewish world,
barely able to imagine what the sight of the Temple would
be like. After a journey of days, weeks, or even longer, however, they would climb the stairs leading to the southern
wall of the Temple, where two giant gateways ushered them
into the Temple precinct. The one to the right was the entrance; the one to the left, the exit.

From the top of the stairs the worshippers had a marvelous view of the city. In front, the southern wall of the
Temple rose majestically before them. Behind, was the area
called the Ophel, a steep slope heading back down into the
Kidron Valley. To the west worshippers could see the lower
city, where David once had ruled. Up above the thousand-
year-old lower city, the upper city sat like a crown, sparkling
with mansions and palaces. To the east was a spectacular
view of the southern side of the Mount of Olives, where the
sun baked down on the thickly gnarled trunks of olive trees.

Climbing up the southern staircase, our ancestors
would traverse a walkway that actually sat upon the roofs of
interconnecting stores that had been built underneath. They
would have visited the stores the day before perhaps, pur-
chasing livestock and fowl for sacrifices or otherwise doing
what pilgrims do to this very day: changing money, sightsee-
ing through the shops, and buying mementos to bring back

home. During the pilgrimage festivals (Pesach, Shavuot, and Sukkot) the lucky ones—with money to rent lodging and foresight to arrive early—filled the inns and extra rooms of private homes that served as antiquity's bed and breakfast places. Vast masses, however, slept outside the city or in the public places under the clear and star-lit sky, thinking, perhaps, of the challenge and ensuing promise that God made to Abraham, "Go forth from your native land to the land that I will show you.... Look toward heaven and count the stars. So shall your offspring be" (Genesis 12:1; 15:5).

Approach

For almost 2,000 years, this access to the Temple precinct was closed. The Temple was destroyed in 70 C.E., and after the Bar Kokhba Revolt in 135 C.E. the Roman emperor, Hadrian, turned the entire old city of Jerusalem into a center for pagan worship, banning Jews from even being here. Eventually the sands of time covered up the entry way, leaving only the western wall available to pilgrims.

But people remembered how Jewish hearts had yearned to be in just this place. Unable to climb the stairs in person, they dreamed of being here every time they prayed. Our sixteenth-century source of Jewish law, the *Shulchan Arukh,* encoded people's yearning this way:

> When rising for prayer outside the Land of Israel, it is customary to face eastward toward the Land and direct our thoughts toward Jerusalem, the Temple, and the Holy of Holies. People who live in the Land should face Jerusalem, and fix their thoughts on the Temple and the Holy of Holies. If they inhabit Jerusalem, they should face the Temple and direct their thoughts toward the Holy of Holies.

Only in our time has archeology cleared away the debris of centuries and allowed us modern pilgrims to do what our ancestors did: to ascend the Temple stairs and stand in the spot where Jews long ago said they met God most regularly, most certainly, and most profoundly. Who knows what meeting lies in wait for us as well?

Acknowledgment

(To be recited while ascending the steps of the southern wall)

Psalm 122

שִׁיר הַמַּעֲלוֹת לְדָוִד
שָׂמַחְתִּי בְּאֹמְרִים לִי
בֵּית יְהֹוָה נֵלֵךְ :
עֹמְדוֹת הָיוּ רַגְלֵינוּ בִּשְׁעָרַיִךְ
יְרוּשָׁלָ͏ִם :
יְרוּשָׁלַ͏ִם הַבְּנוּיָה כְּעִיר שֶׁחֻבְּרָה-
לָּהּ יַחְדָּו :
שֶׁשָּׁם עָלוּ שְׁבָטִים
שִׁבְטֵי-יָהּ
עֵדוּת לְיִשְׂרָאֵל
לְהֹדוֹת לְשֵׁם יְהֹוָה :
כִּי שָׁמָּה | יָשְׁבוּ כִסְאוֹת לְמִשְׁפָּט
כִּסְאוֹת לְבֵית דָּוִיד :
שַׁאֲלוּ שְׁלוֹם יְרוּשָׁלָ͏ִם
יִשְׁלָיוּ אֹהֲבָיִךְ :
יְהִי-שָׁלוֹם בְּחֵילֵךְ
שַׁלְוָה בְּאַרְמְנוֹתָיִךְ :
לְמַעַן אַחַי וְרֵעָי
אֲדַבְּרָה-נָּא שָׁלוֹם בָּךְ :
לְמַעַן בֵּית-יְהֹוָה אֱלֹהֵינוּ
אֲבַקְשָׁה טוֹב לָךְ :

A Song of Ascents. Of David.
I rejoiced when they said to me,
"We are going to the house of our God."
Our feet stood inside your gates, O Jerusalem.
Jerusalem built up, a city knit together,
To which tribes would make pilgrimage,
  the tribes of our God,
    to praise God's name.
There the thrones of judgement stood,
  the thrones of the house of David.
Pray for the peace of Jerusalem;
"May those who love you know well-being.
May there be peace within your ramparts,
  well-being in your citadels.
On behalf of my family and my friends,
I invoke your inner peace."

155

Afterthoughts

Mount Scopus

I declare the Hebrew University opened.

—*Lord Balfour, 1925*

Anticipation

When the War of Independence ended in 1949, Mount Scopus remained an island of Jewish settlement surrounded by hostile Jordanian forces. It had been courageously defended, as its high ground, immediately east of Jerusalem, presented a military advantage. In addition, it had already achieved international fame because of two institutions that dominated its heights: the old Hadassah Hospital and Hebrew University. Health and education were the much sought-after goals of even the earliest settlers.

To the west, Mount Scopus provides the most spectacular view of old Jerusalem. Poet Yehudah Karni wrote, "I saw Jerusalem from Mount Scopus, and she was perfect and whole, little but limitless, contained but not contained." To stand on Mount Scopus today is to experience the non-containment of the Jewish dream, and the limitless capacity of the human soul: in one direction, the most advanced concern for the life of medicine and the mind, and in the other, the vast expanse of Jerusalem, alive with history and beauty.

Approach

It is the midst of World War I in Germany. The father, a successful entrepreneur, ardently supports the Kaiser. His oldest son, Werner, is a Marxist, jailed for fomenting anti-war activity. His younger son, Gershom, age 20, is a Zionist, who helped Werner distribute peace pamphlets, and as a consequence, returned home one day to find a special-delivery eviction notice from his patriotic father. Gershom Scholem would someday, singlehandedly, bring to the world's attention the wisdom of Jewish mysticism. One of young Gershom's early mentors was Martin Buber, and as an adult, he went for long walks with Nobel poet S.Y. Agnon and poet laureate Chaim Nachman Bialik. They all moved to Jerusalem eventually, and typified the Jewish intellectuals who walked the streets of Mount Scopus and created the Hebrew University in 1925.

"There was enormous hospitality," recalls Scholem. "Everyone visited everyone. When you went out, you left the house open. It did not occur to us that there might be a theft. There was, in fact, no stealing, but when we returned, someone was often lying in your bed—the friend of a friend who had been given our address and wanted to spend the night."

As for the university, he remembers the day in 1925 when it opened. "Lord Balfour, the author of the Balfour Declaration, as well as greats of the Zionist movement from Weizmann to Rabbi Kook to Bialik to Achad Ha'am, sat on the tribune of the amphitheater, which had been carved out of the rock of Mount Scopus only a short time previously. I can still picture the old magnificent looking Lord Balfour standing before the setting sun and delivering his eulogy of the Jewish People, its achievements in the past and its hopes in the future."

General Allenby, representing His Majesty's Government, later recalled, "We were in a precarious position in every way. Dr. Weizmann, however, made light of this. Within the hearing of gunshot, he laid the foundation for the university." And after he had done so, Weizmann remembered, "We sang *Hatikvah* and *God Save the King*. But no one seemed anxious to leave and we stood silent with bowed heads while the twilight deepened into night."[30]

Acknowledgment

(To be recited or sung from atop Mt. Scopus, looking down on the Old City.)

From Atop Mt. Scopus, A. Hameiri

מֵעַל פִּסְגַּת הַר הַצּוֹפִים

אֶשְׁתַּחֲוֶה לָךְ אַפָּיִם.

מֵעַל פִּסְגַּת הַר הַצּוֹפִים

שָׁלוֹם לָךְ יְרוּשָׁלַיִם.

מֵאָה דּוֹרוֹת חָלַמְתִּי עָלַיִךְ

לִזְכּוֹת לִרְאוֹת בְּאוֹר פָּנַיִךְ.

יְרוּשָׁלַיִם, יְרוּשָׁלַיִם,

הָאִירִי פָּנַיִךְ לִבְנֵךְ.

יְרוּשָׁלַיִם, יְרוּשָׁלַיִם,

מֵחָרְבוֹתַיִךְ אֶבְנֵךְ.

From atop Mt. Scopus,
I bow down to you, Jerusalem.
From atop Mt. Scopus,
Shalom to you, Jerusalem.
For one hundred generations, have I dreamed of you,
privileged to gaze upon the light of your counte-
nance.

Jerusalem, Jerusalem, light up your face for your
child.
Jerusalem, Jerusalem, from your ruins, I will rebuild
you.

בָּרוּךְ אַתָּה יְיָ אֱלֹהֵינוּ מֶלֶךְ הָעוֹלָם

שֶׁנָּתַן מֵחָכְמָתוֹ לְבָשָׂר וָדָם.

Barukh atah Adonai Eloheinu melekh ha'olam,
shenatan meichokhmato l'vasar vadam.

Blessed is God, for extending wisdom to human
beings.[31]

Afterthoughts

The Valleys of Jerusalem

Yea though I walk through the valley
of the shadow of death,
I will fear no evil. . . .

—*Psalm 23:4*

Anticipation

We normally think of the world's heights as a source of inspiration. But Jerusalem is surrounded by valleys, most of them famous, all of them moving beyond measure. Geography, like life itself, impresses us with its heights only if we know its depths. Take the Valley of Jehoshaphat that separates

ISRAEL—A SPIRITUAL TRAVEL GUIDE

the Mount of Olives from the Golden Gate at Jerusalem's east end. The prophet Joel exclaimed, "When I restore the fortunes of Judah and Jerusalem, I will gather all the nations and bring them into the Valley of Jehoshaphat" (Joel 4:1–2). And ever since then, it was assumed that the messianic era would be ushered in here. The most awesome is perhaps the extension of the Jehoshaphat Valley, the Valley of Kidron, where Absalom's tomb (among others going back centuries) is etched into the silent walls. And the most infamous is *Gehinom*, the Valley of Hinnom, where child sacrifice was practiced and whose name therefore became synonymous with Hell itself. No pilgrimage is complete without at least a short while spent in the depths of Jerusalem's valleys, knowing what prompted the psalmist in the depth of despair to say, "Out of the depths, I cry unto You, O God." But we should also realize what moved Ezekiel to see dead bones rising from the very bowels of the earth, perhaps the most well-known symbol of national resurrection and emblematic of Jewish hopes made real in Israel today.

Approach

From Ezekiel 37

The hand of the Lord came upon me. He took me out and set me down in the valley. It was full of bones. He led me all around them. There were very many of them spread over the valley and they were very dry.

He said to me, "O mortal, can these bones live again?"

I replied, "O Lord God, only You know."

And he said to me, "Prophesy over these bones and say to them, 'O dry bones, hear the word of the Lord! Thus said the Lord God to these bones: I will cause breath to enter you and you shall live again. I will lay sinews upon you and cover you with flesh and form skin over you. And I will put breath into you, and you shall live again. And you shall know that I am the Lord.'"

I prophesied as I had been commanded and while I was prophesying, suddenly there was a sound of rattling, and the bones came together, bone to matching bone. I looked and there were sinews on them, and flesh had grown, and skin had formed over them; but there was no breath in them.

Then He said to me, "Prophesy to the breath. Prophesy O mortal. Say to the breath, 'Thus said the Lord God: Come O breath from the four winds and breathe into these slain, that they may live again.'"

I prophesied as He had commanded me. The breath entered them, and they came to life and stood on their feet a vast multitude.

And He said to me, "O mortal, these bones are the whole house of Israel. They say, 'Our bones are dried up; our hope is gone; we are doomed.' Prophesy, therefore, and say to them, 'Thus said the Lord God: I am going to open your graves and lift you out of the graves, O my people, and bring you to the Land of Israel.'"

Acknowledgment

(To be said while walking through one of Jerusalem's surrounding valleys.)

בָּרוּךְ אַתָּה יְיָ אֱלֹהֵינוּ מֶלֶךְ הָעוֹלָם
הַמַּחֲזִיר נְשָׁמוֹת לִפְגָרִים מֵתִים.

*Barukh atah Adonai Eloheinu melekh ha'olam,
hamachazir n'shamot lif'garim meitim.*

Blessed is God, who restores souls to bodies already dead.[32]

Afterthoughts

Yad Vashem

And Job . . . said, "Let the day perish
on which I was born . . ."

—Job 3:2–3

Anticipation

On July 27, 1946, the Nuremberg Trials drew to a close. Hitler, Himmler, Goebbels and several others who perpetrated the single most chilling mass murder in all of history were all dead. But many were not: Hermann Goering had served for a long time as Hitler's right-hand man; Wilhelm Frick, the Minister of the Interior, had drafted Germany's first anti-Semitic laws that had, bit by bit, stripped Jews of civil rights and all means of employment. Hans Frank had overseen the mass destruction of Polish Jewry; Alfred Rosenberg had masterminded the Nazi ideology of Jew-hatred; Baldur von Schirach had orchestrated the indoctrination of Hitler Youth; Fritz Saikel had overseen slave labor recruitment. On the morning of July 27, Sir Hartley Shawcross rose to conclude his trial summation for the prosecution.

He began with an eyewitness account of a mass execution by one of the *Einsatzgruppen*, the select commando teams used to eradicate Jewish communities in towns overrun by the German army. Those in attendance had already heard ten months of chilling testimony. Yet there could not have been a dry eye even in that hardened audience, as Shawcross described the murder of a thousand or more people—men, women and children—who were herded in groups of twenty-five into a pit and systematically shot by "an SS man who sat on the edge of the pit, a tommy gun on his lap, and smoking a cigarette." The account described some of the victims—ordinary folk, really—like a "father holding the hand of a boy about ten years old and speaking to him softly. The boy was fighting his tears. The father pointed to the sky, stroked his head and seemed to explain something to him."

At the end Shawcross challenged the jury with these words:

> Mankind itself—struggling now to reestablish in all the countries of the world the common simple things—liberty, love, understanding—comes to this court and cries, "These are our laws, let them prevail!" You will remember when you come to give your decision the story of the mass execution, in a determination that these things shall not occur again. The father—you remember—pointed to the sky, and seemed to say something to his boy.

Approach

A Dream, Yitzchak Katzenelson[33]

חֲלוֹם חָלַמְתִּי נוֹרָא מְאֹד —
אֵין עַמִּי, עַמִּי אֵינֶנּוּ עוֹד;
בִּצְעָקָה קַמְתִּי — אֲהָהּ! אֲהָהּ!
אֲשֶׁר חָלַמְתִּי, בָּא לִי, בָּא!
"הָהּ, אֵל בָּרְמָהּ!" אֶקְרָא רְתֵת:
"עַל מָה וְלָמָה עַמִּי מֵת?!
עַל מָה וְלָמָה מֵת לַשָּׁוְא?
לֹא בַּמִּלְחָמָה, לֹא בַּקְּרָב ...
נְעָרִים, זְקֵנִים, גַּם נָשִׁים וָטָף
כְּבָר אֵינָם, אֵינָם — סְפְּקוּ כָּף!"
כֹּה אֶבְךְ בִּיגוֹנִי, גַּם יוֹם, גַּם לֵיל —
עַל מָה רִבּוֹנִי? וְלָמָה אֵלִי?

A dream I dreamt of terrible woe,
My people gone, alive no more.
I arose, with a shout: "Oh no!, Oh no!"
The dream I dreamt—It has become so!
"O God on high," shuddering, I cry,
"My people, dead! Wherefore and why?
Wherefore and why? In vain they died,
Not in war, fighting for their lives,

The young, the old, even wife and child,
They are no more—lament the sorrow!
All day, all night, I weep and cry,
Wherefore, O God? Why, Adonai?"

Acknowledgment

A Service of Memorial for the Six Million

(The following set of prayers may be said alone or as part of a group. They are probably best recited in the Valley of Communities, near the memorial for a community that has some significance for people in the group. When the service is over, individuals may wish to find the marker for a community where members of their own family perished, and to repeat the two central memorial prayers below—*Yizkor* and *El malei rachamim*—at that spot.)

(Reader)

We now testify to what once was,
And call to mind the people who died in a time
when evil walked the face of the earth.
They are no more.

(In the following two memorial prayers, you may insert the names of any you know who perished in the *Shoah*.)

(Silent Meditation)

Yizkor... *("May God remember...")*

יִזְכּוֹר אֱלֹהִים נִשְׁמוֹת יַקִּירַי ... שֶׁהָלְכוּ לְעוֹלָמָם.
אָנָּא תִּהְיֶינָה נַפְשׁוֹתֵיהֶם צְרוּרוֹת בִּצְרוֹר הַחַיִּים
וּתְהִי מְנוּחָתָם כָּבוֹד.
שֹׂבַע שְׂמָחוֹת אֶת פָּנֶיךָ,
נְעִימוֹת בִּימִינְךָ נֶצַח. אָמֵן.

May God remember (my dear ones _____)
and our brothers and sisters of the House of Israel
who gave their lives
for the sanctification of the divine name.
May they be at one with the One

who is life eternal.
May the beauty of their lives shine for evermore,
and may my life always bring honor to their memory.

(Reader, or, if possible, chanted in the traditional manner)

El malei rachamim . . .
("O God, full of compassion . . .")

אֵל מָלֵא רַחֲמִים שׁוֹכֵן בַּמְּרוֹמִים,
הַמְצֵא מְנוּחָה נְכוֹנָה תַּחַת כַּנְפֵי הַשְּׁכִינָה
עִם קְדוֹשִׁים וּטְהוֹרִים
כְּזֹהַר הָרָקִיעַ מַזְהִירִים לְנִשְׁמוֹת יַקִּירֵינוּ שֶׁהָלְכוּ
לְעוֹלָמָם.
בַּעַל הָרַחֲמִים יַסְתִּירֵם בְּסֵתֶר כְּנָפָיו לְעוֹלָמִים,
וְיִצְרוֹר בִּצְרוֹר הַחַיִּים אֶת נִשְׁמוֹתֵיהֶם. יְיָ הוּא נַחֲלָתָם.
וְיָנוּחוּ בְשָׁלוֹם עַל מִשְׁכְּבוֹתֵיהֶם,
וְנֹאמַר: אָמֵן.

O God full of compassion, eternal spirit of the uni-
verse,
grant perfect rest under the wings of your presence
to all our brothers and sisters who have entered eter-
nity.
Source of mercy: Let them find refuge for ever
in the shadow of your wings,
and let their souls be bound up in the bond of eter-
nal life.
The eternal God is their inheritance.
May they rest in peace;
And let us say:Amen.[34]

(Reader)

The memories of their shattered lives are woven in
our tapestry of history,
With blood-soaked reds and ghostly whites that will
not go away.
Sunrise yellow, autumn leaves, and deep blue skies
of every day
Must now compete for our attention.

Perhaps the colored blotches of our tortured past
will eventually fade,

Their threads run out.
Listen to Isaiah:

(All together)

Take comfort then, take comfort, O my people, says
your God. Speak tenderly to Jerusalem; proclaim to
her that her bondage is over, her iniquity pardoned.
She has received ample punishment.

(Reader)

We are the weavers now, entrusted with tomorrow's
*   choice of wools.*
Yellow can be sunflowers too—not just Auschwitz
*   badges.*
Sky-blue, blossom-pink, and Mediterranean-green:
that, I tell you, is the world that God created:
And that too is our history, just as much as chimney
*   gray.*

Let us leave this place sobered by our memories,
But thankful for today,
And hopeful for tomorrow.

(All together)

How greatly we are blessed.
How wondrous is our lot.
How beautiful our heritage.[35]

As every day for centuries,
We have celebrated life,
And declared God one.

שְׁמַע יִשְׂרָאֵל יְיָ אֱלֹהֵינוּ יְיָ אֶחָד.

Sh'ma Yisrael Adonai Eloheinu Adonai Echad.

Hear O Israel, Adonai is our God, Adonai is one.

בָּרוּךְ אַתָּה יְיָ אֱלֹהֵינוּ מֶלֶךְ הָעוֹלָם זוֹכֵר הַנִּשְׁכָּחוֹת.

Barukh atah Adonai Eloheinu melekh ha'olam,
zokher hanishkakhot.

Blessed is God who remembers.[36]

Afterthoughts

Yemin Moshe (at The Windmill)

From Moses to Moses, there was no one like Moses.

—Folklore

Anticipation

There have been many men named Moses in our history.
At Yemin Moshe you will celebrate the memory of one of
them: Moses Montefiore (1784–1885), possibly the most famous British Jew of all time. By the age of forty, he had made
a fortune as one of only twelve "Jew brokers" (as they were
known) in the city of London. He had also married into the
Rothschild family. He devoted the rest of his life to Jewish
causes, sparked in large part by something like a conversion-
ary experience on his first visit to *Eretz Yisrael,* in 1827.

Though relatively unobservant as a Jew until then, he
returned home to England on fire with Jewish commitment
and spent the rest of his life as an Orthodox Jew. In 1840, he
intervened on behalf of his own British government to save
the lives of Jews in Damascus who were being charged with
ritual murder. He was later knighted and named a baron for
his humanitarian efforts on behalf of the Jewish People.

Sanitary conditions in old Jerusalem were deplorable
at the time—with open sewers, unpaved streets, scattered
garbage, and even dead animals lying decomposed along the
dusty narrow roadways. British missionaries were establishing
a hospital there which would take care of Jerusalem's Jewish
population, while also introducing them to the Christian
message. Jews had been trying to establish their own hospital as well. The most serious attempt, however, had been the
initiative of Reform Rabbi Ludwig Phillipson, and when
Jerusalem's Orthodox rabbis found out that he was Reform,
they quashed the project. Montefiore, who was Orthodox,
was able to revive the project under his own name. His plans
were given a sudden boost when philanthropist Judah Touro
of Newport, Rhode Island died, leaving $60,000 for his
"unfortunate Jewish brethren in the Holy Land" and Montefiore as administrator.

In 1855, Montefiore made his fourth visit to Jerusalem, this time with money in his pocket to establish a hospital just outside the crowded city's walls. He hoped also to initiate a healthy rural agricultural settlement there. The hospital never materialized, partly because the French branch of the Rothschilds decided to build one on their own, and partly because of feuding among the Jerusalem rabbis. The agricultural effort died also. But his settlement remains, its very name, Yemin Moshe, "The Right Hand of Moses" (a reference borrowed from Isaiah 63:12), recalling its patron-founder. And the old windmill is still there, a charming memento of a time gone by.[37]

Approach

The Windmill in Yemin Moshe,
Yehuda Amichai

This windmill never ground flour.
It ground holy air and Bialik's
Birds of longing, it ground
Words and ground time, it ground
Rain and even shells
But it never ground flour.

Now it's discovered us,
And grinds our lives day by day,
Making out of us the flour of peace,
Making out of us the bread of peace,
For the generation to come.

Acknowledgment

(To be recited while standing in front of the windmill.)

בָּרוּךְ אַתָּה יְיָ אֱלֹהֵינוּ מֶלֶךְ הָעוֹלָם מַשִׁיב הָרוּחַ.

Barukh atah Adonai Eloheinu melekh ha'olam,
mashiv haru'ach.

Blessed is God who makes the wind blow.[38]

Afterthoughts

Mount Nebo

Who shall ascend the mountain of the Lord?

—*Psalm 29:3*

This refers to Moses, as it is said,
"And Moses went up to God" (Exodus 19:3).

—*Midrash to the last chapter of Deuteronomy*

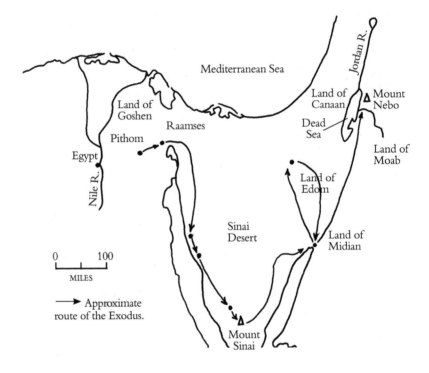

Anticipation

The Israelites were never a sea people. When they left Egypt, they could hardly embark on ships and cross the Mediterranean to one of the ports on Israel's western coast. But they did not take the direct land route either, hugging the Mediterranean's southern coast until they reached their destination. Our best guess is that after crossing the northern tip of the Red Sea, they turned south and wandered the Sinai desert for a proverbial forty years, then turned north again, and entered Israel from the east through what is now the Kingdom of Jordan. Many biblical sites are therefore not in Israel at all, but in the land once populated by the Ammonites, Amorites, Moabites and other peoples through whose territory the Israelites passed on their way home. Of all these sites, the Bible recalls with special affection Mount Nebo. It was there that Moses died, after being granted his last look at the land to which he had faithfully led his people, but which he would never enter.

The midrash (Deuteronomy *Rabbah*) remembers his last minutes this way:

> Upon hearing of the decree that Moses would die without entering Israel, the angels objected, but in vain. God descended in person to do the deed, and said, "Moses, fold your eyelids over your eyes." And he did so. Then God said, "Place your hands upon your breast," and he did so. So God said, "Put your feet next to one another," and he did so.
>
> God then summoned Moses' soul, explaining, "You were assigned to Moses' body for 120 years. The time is up. You may now leave."
>
> But the soul objected, "You created me and You formed me; You breathed me into Moses' body for 120 years. All that is true. But could there be a purer body than that of Moses? I love him and do not want to leave."
>
> "Soul," God replied, "I will raise you to the highest heaven where you will occupy a place of special grandeur. Do not fear. But the time has come. You must leave."
>
> Still the soul resisted, saying one last time, "I beg of You, let me remain forever in the body of Moses."
>
> God saw and understood, but there was nothing God could do. Stooping low upon the bed where Moses lay, God gave Moses a kiss and took the soul away with a kiss. Then God wept, as did the heavens and the earth, and all the ministering angels. All of Israel joined the angels in mourning, saying, "He shall come to peace; those who walk in uprightness shall have rest" (Isaiah 57:2). "The memory of the righteous shall be a blessing" (Proverbs 10:7).

Approach

The Death of Moses (Deuteronomy 34:1–12)

Moses went up from the steps of Moab to Mt. Nebo, to the summit of Pisgah, opposite Jericho, and the Lord showed him the whole land; Gilead as far as Dan; all of Naphtali; the land of Ephraim and Manasseh; the whole land of Judah as far as the Mediterranean; the Negev; and the plain—the Valley of Jericho, the city of palm trees—as far as Zoar. And the Lord said to him, "This is the land of which I swore to Abraham, Isaac and Jacob, I will give it to your offspring. I have let you see it with your own eyes, but you shall not cross there."

So Moses, the servant of the Lord, died there, in the land of Moab, at the command of the Lord. He buried him in the valley in the land of Moab, near Beth-Pe'or, and no one knows his burial place to this day. Moses was a hundred and twenty years old when he died; his eyes were undimmed and his vigor unabated. And the Israelites bewailed Moses in the steppes of Moab for thirty days.

The wailing period in the mourning of Moses came to an end. Now Joshua the son of Nun was filled with the spirit of wisdom because Moses had laid his hands on him; and the Israelites heeded him, doing as the Lord had commanded Moses.

Never again did there arise in Israel a prophet like Moses, whom the Lord singled out face to face, for the various signs and portents that the Lord sent him to display in the land of Egypt, against Pharaoh and all his courtiers and his whole country, and for all the great might and awesome power that Moses displayed before all Israel.

Acknowledgment

The righteousness which you have taught is
eternal justice; your Torah is truth.
Your righteousness extends throughout the universe.
Your deeds reflect your greatness, incomparable God.

Your righteousness is like the lofty mountains; your
judgements like the great deep;
humankind and animals are in your care; help them
God.

—Psalms 119:142, 71:19, 36:7[39]

בָּרוּךְ אַתָּה יְיָ דַּיַּן הָאֱמֶת.

Barukh atah Adonai, dayyan ha'emet.

Blessed is God, the true judge.[40]

Afterthoughts

Hebron and Bethlehem: Tombs of the Matriarchs and Patriarchs

God of Abraham, God of Isaac, God of Jacob, God of Sarah,
God of Rebekah, God of Rachel, God of Leah. . . .

—The daily liturgy: Kol Haneshamah
(the Reconstructionist prayer book)

(At this writing, it is not clear whether it is possible or advisable to visit the sites where the Bible says our Matriarchs and Patriarchs are buried. Political considerations may make such a visit physically dangerous, and inadvisable from the perspective of Israel's relationship with its Arab neighbors. But in the hope that a secure and lasting peace will open Hebron and Bethlehem to Jewish pilgrimage, the following ritual is provided.)

Anticipation

Jewish life before the descent into Egypt occurred very mainly in what is now the Arab territory east of Jerusalem. Only after the Exodus did the focus of our national destiny shift slowly westward to Jerusalem and the Mediterranean. "Home" for our bedouin-like forebears, from Abraham and Sarah to Jacob, Rachel and Leah, was likely a campsite in what is now the West Bank. If there had been a capital city at the time, it might have been Hebron or even Bethlehem, not Jerusalem. All but one of our earliest ancestors are buried in Hebron. The exception, Rachel, is buried in Bethlehem.

> Abraham buried Sarah his wife in the cave of the field of Machpelah facing Mamre, which is Hebron (Genesis 23:19).

> Rachel was in childbirth and had a hard labor. When her labor was at its hardest, the midwife said to her, "Have no fear, for it is another boy for you." As she was breathing her last—for she was dying—

179

ISRAEL—A SPIRITUAL TRAVEL GUIDE

she named him Ben Oni, but his father called him
Benjamin. Thus Rachel died. She was buried on the
road to Ephrat—now Bethlehem. Over her grave,
Jacob set up a pillar; it is the pillar at Rachel's grave
to this day (Genesis 35:16-20).

Jacob instructed his children, "I am about to die,
Bury me with my fathers in the cave which is in the
field of Ephron the Hittite, the cave which is in the
field of Machpelah, facing Mamre, in the Land of
Canaan, the field that Abraham bought from Ephron the Hittite for a burial site. There Abraham and
his wife Sarah were buried; there Isaac and his wife
Rebekah were buried; and there I buried Leah"
(Genesis 49:29-33).

Approach

Our Rabbis say that Jacob never died. Just his body lies inside the sepulcher, not his soul, for it is written, "Jacob was
gathered to his people," not "Jacob died." Somehow his soul
carried on, and still is felt like a tangible presence by us, his
children, appropriately named *B'nai Yisrael*, Children of Israel, that is, "children of Jacob" whose other name was Israel,
after all. His body gave out as he was blessing his twelve sons,
the progenitors of the tribes of Israel, and therefore of us—
as it is written, "Each according to his blessing, he blessed
them." That means, say the Rabbis, that none of them received a blessing that was the same as the others; and so too,
each of us is blessed in our own uniqueness. The way to
know our blessing is to encounter the soul of Jacob, who
will touch us softly as if with patriarch-hands, and whisper
to us of our destiny.

Rachel too never really died, the Rabbis say, for it is
written, "A cry is heard, wailing, bitter weeping, Rachel
weeping for her children," to which God responds (anticipating Israel today), "They shall return. Your children shall
return to their country" (Jeremiah 31:15). On their way to
exile, Jews passed through Bethlehem to be embraced by
Mother Rachel. So too with us; when estranged from all
that is holy we know that Rachel our mother weeps for us,
and rocks us gently in her arms.

From the tombs of our ancestors it is possible to feel the hands of Jacob and the arms of Rachel. It is possible to know with certainty that we are blessed and we are loved.

Acknowledgment

(The grave site of matriarchs and patriarchs presents an opportunity to pray for blessing for those we love most. The following prayer provides a space to insert the name(s) of those for whom you wish to invoke blessing. It may be said in Hebrew or in English. If the one whom you wish to bless is present, it is appropriate to place your hands on his or her shoulders or head while saying the blessing.)

מִי שֶׁבֵּרַךְ אֲבוֹתֵינוּ אַבְרָהָם יִצְחָק וְיַעֲקֹב

וְאִמוֹתֵינוּ שָׂרָה רִבְקָה רָחֵל וְלֵאָה

הוּא יְבָרֵךְ אֶת _____.

Mi sheberakh avoteinu avraham yitzchak
   v'ya'akov

V'imoteinu sarah, rivkah, rachel v'leah
hu y'varekh et _____ .

May the One who blessed Abraham, Isaac and
   Jacob,
Sarah Rebekah, Rachel and Leah,
Also bless _____.

God grant (you/him/her/them) a long life, a peaceful life with goodness and blessing, sustenance and physical vitality, a life informed by purity and piety, a life free from shame and reproach, a life of abundance and honor, a life embracing piety and love of Torah, a life in which (your/his/her/their) heart's desires for goodness will be fulfilled.

(You may pause and add your own words of blessing here.)

Amen.[41]

Afterthoughts

THE COASTAL PLAIN:
"Yamah—to the West"

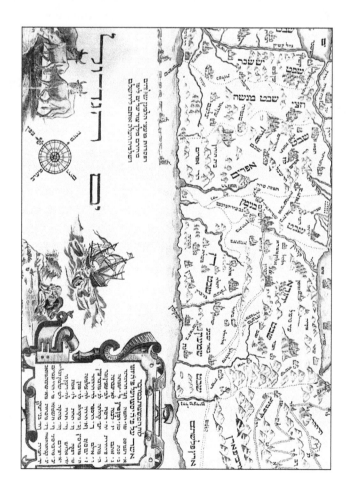

The Mediterranean

The sea is God's; God made it.

—Psalm 95:5

Anticipation

"In the beginning God created the heaven and the earth" (Genesis 1:1). That was Day One, some 4.5 *billion* years ago, the scientists say.

The "wild beasts of every kind" (Genesis 1:24) didn't arrive for another four billion years, and we humans are relative newcomers, born 2.5 million years ago. "God created man ... male and female" (Genesis 1:27) but only when Day Six drew to an end. It took another 2 million years for those early human beings to look like us, and nearly half a million more for us to start counting "history."

By then our ancestors had discovered the Mediterranean. Abraham and Sarah got there from the East, about 2000 B.C.E. Joseph kept his brothers alive because as the mighty Nile River meets the Mediterranean, it forms a flood plain (like the Mississippi Delta) making food plentiful. By the year 975 B.C.E., King David had carved out a Jewish state, but to do so, he had to fight the Philistines, Mediterranean marauders whose ships set down on the shore of what is now the Gaza strip. Later still, the Mediterranean supported the navies of Alexander the Great and Julius Caesar. And just yesterday, as it were, the Islamic empire sailed its breadth and settled all of North Africa and even Spain.

Until 800 C.E., when Charlemagne developed European culture far away in land-locked France, most western men and women could not have imagined life outside the Mediterranean. At first, they had called it *Mare Nostrum,* Latin for "Our Sea." A third-century geographer named Solinus named it "Mediterranean"—"The Sea in the Middle of the Earth." Is it any wonder that the Rabbis recited a blessing for this sea of seas, the *Yam Hagadol,* or "Great Sea"?

Stand at the beach and watch the clear blue waves roll in much as people did when history first began. Our biblical author had this in mind when he remembered God saying on Day Two, "Let the water below the sky be gathered into one area" (Genesis 1:9).

Get there in time to watch the sun set, if you can, a pristine sight that hasn't changed since God said, "Let there be lights in the expanse of the sky" (Genesis 1:14). Some things are forever.

Approach

O God, My God, Hannah Szenes

אֵלִי אֵלִי
שֶׁלֹּא יִגָּמֵר לְעוֹלָם
הַחוֹל וְהַיָּם
רִשְׁרוּשׁ שֶׁל הַמַּיִם
בְּרַק הַשָּׁמַיִם תְּפִלַּת הָאָדָם.

O God, my God,
I pray that these things never end:
The sand and the sea,
The rush of the waters,
The crash of the heaven,
the prayer of the heart.

Acknowledgment

בָּרוּךְ אַתָּה יְיָ אֱלֹהֵינוּ מֶלֶךְ הָעוֹלָם
שֶׁעָשָׂה אֶת הַיָּם הַגָּדוֹל.

Barukh atah Adonai, Eloheinu melekh ha'olam,
she'asah et hayam hagadol.

Blessed is God, who made the Great Sea.[42]

Afterthoughts

Haifa—Mount Carmel

The city of the future . . .

—*Theodor Herzl*

Anticipation

Haifa is Israel's garden city. The road winds up from the beach through three levels of terraced dwellings, including "Carmel," named after the mountain on which the city rests. Its roots are ancient, prehistoric probably, but it has come into its own only in modern times as Israel's chief port. Still, the marks of history, old and new, are strikingly evident, especially in the city's southern approach from Tel Aviv. As the road curves around you see the mountain standing stark before you on the right; here Elijah fought the prophets of Ba'al, then fled King Ahab and Queen Jezebel, and journeyed south to the wilderness where he could hear "the still small voice" of God.

On the left is the remains of a ship (like the famous *Exodus*) which carried illegal immigrants (*M'apilim*) from Hitler's infernos, and then from post-war Displaced Persons camps, past watchful coast guards into British Palestine. The image of illegal ships breaking past the barricades runs deep in the older generation, not only here in Israel, but for all Jews alive at the time. Jews who survived the concentration camps were summarily interned once again behind barbed wire on Cyprus. By 1947, two full years after the liberation from Hitler, the Cyprus camps were full and getting fuller, to the point where a Passover Haggadah was issued in Tel Aviv for the detainees to use. On its cover was the image of the refugee ship, a promise of what was to come with Israeli independence in 1948: a final trip home, landing here in Haifa harbor, this time legally, with the spirit of Elijah looking down from Mount Carmel, as if the first steps toward messianic deliverance were really at hand.

Yehuda-Leib Cohen captures the flavor of the countryside where history and nature meet in mystical embrace,
and where Elijah may not be the only spirit you encounter.

Upon My Death, Yehuda-Leib Cohen

Upon my death—
Remember that I loved
The Carmel at sunset. . . .

Remember that I loved
plants sprouting through stones on a spring day,
and moonlit nights,
and playing in the waves on the shore
at the foot of the monastery
in the heat of the afternoon. . . .

Upon my death—
if my body falls into the hands of strangers
Please remember
and look for my spirit
in the Carmel. . . .

Approach

From 1 Kings 18

The word of God came to Elijah in the third year
saying, "Go appear to Ahab. I will send rain upon
the earth."

The famine was severe in Samaria, and Ahab
summoned Obadiah who was in charge of the
palace. (Obadiah was deeply in awe of God. When
Jezebel was killing off the prophets of the Lord,
Obadiah took a hundred prophets, hid them fifty
to a cave, and provided them with bread and water.)
Ahab said to Obadiah, "Go through the land to all
the springs of water and all the wadis; perhaps we
may find grass to keep the horses and the mules
alive, and not lose some of the animals." They divided the land between them, Ahab going alone in
one direction, and Obadiah by himself in the other.

Elijah met Obadiah on the way. When Obadiah

recognized him, he bowed low on the ground, and asked, "Is it you, my lord, Elijah?"

"It is I," he responded, "Go tell your lord that Elijah has arrived. . . ."

When Ahab saw Elijah, he asked, "Is it you, you troubler of Israel?"

He replied, "I have not troubled Israel, but you and your father's house have, for you have forsaken the commandments of Adonai, and followed Ba'al. Now, therefore, assemble all Israel for me at Mount Carmel, with the 450 prophets of Ba'al and the 400 prophets of Asherah, who eat at Jezebel's table."

So Ahab assembled the prophets at Mount Carmel, and Elijah said, "How long will you go limping between two opinions? If Adonai is God, follow Him; if Ba'al is God, follow him." The people would not answer.

Then Elijah said to the people, "I, yes, I alone, am left as a prophet of Adonai, and Ba'al's prophets number 450. Have two bulls brought for us. Let them choose one, dismember it, and lay it on the wood, but put no fire to it. I will prepare the other bull, lay it on the wood, and put no fire to it. Then you call on the name of your god, and I will call on Adonai. The one who answers by fire is God." "Well said," the people replied.

The prophets of Ba'al took their bull, prepared it, and called on the name of Ba'al from morning to noon, crying, "O Ba'al, answer us." But there was no voice and no response. They limped about the altar they had made, until at noon, Elijah taunted them, saying, "Cry loudly. Surely he is God. He may be meditating, or has wandered off, or is on a journey, or is asleep and must be wakened." So they cried aloud, as was their custom, and cut themselves with swords and lances until their blood gushed out all over them. As midday passed, they raved on, but still, there was no voice, no answer, no response at all. . . .

Then Elijah said, "Fill four jars with water and pour it on the offering and on the wood." Then he said, "Do it a second time," and they did. "Do it a third time," he said, and they did it a third time, so that water ran all around the altar and filled the surrounding trench also.

Elijah said, "O Lord, God of Abraham, Isaac and

Israel, make it known today that you are God in Israel." Then the fire of the Lord came down and consumed the burnt offering, the wood, the stones, and the dust, and even consumed the water that was in the trench. . . .

Elijah said to Ahab, "Go up, eat and drink, for there is the sound of rushing rain." So Ahab went up to eat and drink, and Elijah went to the top of Carmel, where he bowed down on the ground, and put his face between his knees. He said to his servant, "Get up and look out toward the sea."

He went and looked, and said, "There is nothing."

"Go again," he said, "seven times."

At the seventh time, he said, "Look, a little cloud no bigger than a person's hand is rising from the sea. . . ."

In a little while, the heavens grew black with clouds and wind, and there was a heavy rain.

Acknowledgment

(At the foot of Mount Carmel, facing the mountain and its caves where Elijah was said to abide:)

May the Almighty again send us Elijah the prophet (may he be remembered for good). And may he bless each and every one of us in God's name. God grant us blessing, life and peace.[43]

מִי שֶׁעָנָה אֶת אֵלִיָּהוּ בְּהַר הַכַּרְמֶל הוּא יַעֲנֶה אוֹתָנוּ.
בָּרוּךְ אַתָּה יְיָ אֱלֹהֵינוּ מֶלֶךְ הָעוֹלָם
מְשַׂמֵּחַ יִשְׂרָאֵל בְּאֵלִיָּהוּ הַנָּבִיא.

*Mi she'anah et eliyahu b'har hacarmel hu
    ya'aneh otanu.
Barukh atah Adonai, Eloheinu melekh ha'olam,
    m'samei'ach yisrael b'eliyahu hanavi.*

May the One who answered Elijah at Mount
    Carmel answer us.
Blessed is God, who gladdens Israel with Elijah
    the prophet.[44]

(At the *M'apilim* ship)

> *For any Jews, still handed over to persecution*
>   *or captivity,*
> *Whether they be stranded on land or on sea,*
> *May God show them mercy,*
> *And bring them out from the straits they are in*
> *To breathing space aplenty,*
> *From darkness to light,*
> *From servitude to freedom,*
> *Speedily and soon,*
> *And let us say,*
> *Amen.* [45]

בָּרוּךְ אַתָּה יְיָ אֱלֹהֵינוּ מֶלֶךְ הָעוֹלָם שׁוֹמֵעַ צְעָקָה.

Barukh atah Adonai Eloheinu melekh ha'olam,
shomei'ah ts'akah.

Blessed is God, who attends to calls for help.[46]

Afterthoughts

Tel Aviv—Beit Hat'futsot
(Museum of the Diaspora)

I came to the exiles of Tel Aviv, who lived by the river . . .

—*Ezekiel 3:15*

Anticipation

> On Saturday, we would go out to survey the tract of
> land which stretched out before us with its golden
> sands while silence and emptiness were all about.
> We ourselves stood bewildered. How would a set-
> tlement arise on these shifting sands; how would
> houses be built and streets drawn? And indeed, there
> were skeptics who prophesied, "When hair grows
> on the palm of my hand, a suburb will arise on these
> sands. And even if you build houses here, the shift-
> ing sands carried from the seashore will soon cover
> them. You will always have to dig yourself out and
> protect yourself against the moving sands."

So wrote one of the original settlers, Rivka Alper, as she rec-
ollected Tel Aviv's origins. Once, this was nothing but sand
dunes, like the ones you cross on your way from the parking
lot to some of the beaches. But in 1909, visionaries came
here from Russia to do the impossible: to erect a city where
there wasn't even any water. They lived in crowded Jaffa,
next-door, and thought they were creating a tiny suburb
which they named *Achuzat Bayit*, meaning "Homestead." As
the city burgeoned, they sought a better name:

> Many meetings and discussions were devoted to this
> issue. Proposed were *Herzliah* (named after Herzl),
> New Jaffa, *Neve Jaffa* ("The beauty of Jaffa"), *Iriyah*
> ("Little City"), *Aviva* ("Spring"), *Yefefiyah* ("Beauty"),
> until Sheinkin (one of the settlers) revealed that
> a name had already been chosen for this place by
> the herald of the Jewish state himself—Herzl, in his
> book, *Altneuland* ("Old-New Land," Herzl's novel

about what a Jewish state would be like). Nachum Sokolow (Zionist thinker, author, and political leader after World War I) had translated it as Tel Aviv.

A *tel* is a mound of earth where antiquity lies buried. *Aviv*, meaning "springtime," connotes just the opposite: not yesterday but tomorrow; life renewed, not memories buried in the sand. Modern Tel Aviv is indeed these opposites: mostly the excitement of tomorrow, but here, at the Museum of the Diaspora, we recollect the past as well.

Approach

Poem Without End, Yehuda Amichai

Inside the brand-new museum
there's an old synagogue.
Inside the synagogue
is me.
Inside me
my heart.
Inside my heart
a museum.
Inside the museum
a synagogue,
inside it
me,
inside me
my heart,
inside my heart
a museum.

Acknowledgment

בָּרוּךְ אַתָּה יְיָ אֱלֹהֵינוּ מֶלֶךְ הָעוֹלָם
מְקַבֵּץ נִדְחֵי עַמּוֹ יִשְׂרָאֵל.

Barukh atah Adonai Eloheinu melekh ha'olam,
m'kabetz nid'chei amo Yisrael.

Blessed is God, who gathers together
the dispersed of the Jewish People.[47]

Afterthoughts

The Guide
to Blessing

or

How to Find Blessing Wherever You Go

They shall plant vineyards and drink their
    wine.
They shall till gardens and eat their fruit.
I will plant them on their soil, nevermore to
    be uprooted,
From the soil I have given them—said Adonai
    your God.

—*Amos 9:14–15*

For a Place of Aliyah Such As a Merkaz K'litah (Absorption Center)

וַתֹּאמֶר צִיּוֹן

עֲזָבַנִי יְיָ

וַאדֹנָי שְׁכֵחָנִי.

הֲתִשְׁכַּח אִשָּׁה עוּלָהּ מֵרַחֵם בֶּן בִּטְנָהּ?

גַּם אֵלֶּה תִשְׁכַּחְנָה

וְאָנֹכִי לֹא אֶשְׁכָּחֵךְ.

מִהֲרוּ בָּנָיִךְ

מְהָרְסַיִךְ וּמַחֲרִיבַיִךְ מִמֵּךְ יֵצֵאוּ.

שְׂאִי סָבִיב עֵינַיִךְ וּרְאִי

כֻּלָּם נִקְבְּצוּ בָאוּ לָךְ.

חַי אָנִי נְאֻם יְיָ כִּי כֻלָּם כַּעֲדִי תִלְבָּשִׁי

וּתְקַשְּׁרִים כַּכַּלָּה.

כִּי חָרְבֹתַיִךְ וְשֹׁמְמֹתַיִךְ

וְאֶרֶץ הֲרִסֻתֵךְ

כִּי עַתָּה תֵּצְרִי מִיּוֹשֵׁב וְרָחֲקוּ מְבַלְּעָיִךְ.

עוֹד יֹאמְרוּ בְאָזְנָיִךְ בְּנֵי שִׁכֻּלָיִךְ

צַר לִי הַמָּקוֹם גְּשָׁה לִּי וְאֵשֵׁבָה.

Isaiah 49: 14–15, 17–20

Zion says,
"Adonai has forsaken me.
Adonai has forgotten me."
Can a woman forget her baby?
or disown the child of her womb?
Though even she might forget,
Your God could never forget you. . . .

Swiftly, your children arrive,
Look all around, and see,
They all assemble, they come to you. . . .

Soon you shall be crowded with settlers,
While destroyers stay far from you.
The children you thought you had lost
Shall yet say in your hearing,
"The place is too crowded for me.
Make room for me to settle."

The Law of Return

(Passed by the Knesset on July 5, 1950, marking the for-
ty-sixth anniversary of Theodor Herzl's death. The law guar-
antees the right of every Jew to settle in Israel.)

Every Jew is entitled to immigrate to Israel. . . . The
rights of a Jew according to this law . . . are trans-
ferred also to a child or grandchild of a Jew or to a
spouse of a Jew and to a spouse of a child or grandchild of a Jew, but exclude a person who has will-
fully converted to another religion.

בָּרוּךְ אַתָּה יְיָ אֱלֹהֵינוּ מֶלֶךְ הָעוֹלָם
הַמּוֹלִיכֵנוּ קוֹמְמִיּוּת לְאַרְצֵנוּ.

Barukh atah Adonai Eloheinu melekh ha'olam,
hamolicheinu kom'miyut l'artsenu.

Blessed is God who leads us upright to our land.[1]

For a Place of Beauty

I Want Always to Have Eyes to See, Natan Zach

I want always to have eyes to see
The world's beauty; and to praise
This marvelous faultless splendor; to praise
The One who made it beautiful to praise,
And full, so very full, and beautiful.
I want never to be blind before

The world—so long as I am alive. I renounce
All other things, but never do I say "Enough
Of seeing this beauty in which I live,
And into which my hands extend like sailing ships
Plotting life's course. . . ."

I will never stop praising; my praise will have no
*   end.*
And when I fall, I will get up again—if only for a
*   moment—let no one say,*
"He fell!"—but, "He got up," for a moment, to
*   praise*
With eyes of hindsight
That for which praise should never cease.

בָּרוּךְ אַתָּה יְיָ אֱלֹהֵינוּ מֶלֶךְ הָעוֹלָם שֶׁכָּכָה לוֹ בְּעוֹלָמוֹ.

Barukh atah Adonai Eloheinu melekh ha'olam,
shekakhah lo b'olamo.

Blessed is God, whose world is like this!

For a Place of Blessing

(It is common at several places in Israel to request a blessing
for those we love, or to offer them such a blessing in person
if they are with us. The following prayer is recommended for
recitation at the graves of the matriarchs and patriarchs, but
may also be said at other, equally appropriate sites, such as
the Tomb of David in Jerusalem, or just at a Shabbat dinner,
wherever it may occur.)

Mi sheberakh avraham yitzchak v'ya'akov
sarah, rivkah, rachel v'leah
hu y'varekh et _____ .

May the One who blessed Abraham, Isaac and
    Jacob,
Sarah, Rebekah, Rachel and Leah,
Also bless _____ .

God grant (you/him/her/them) a long life, a peaceful life with goodness and blessing, sustenance

and physical vitality, a life informed by purity and
piety, a life free from shame and reproach, a life of
abundance and honor, a life embracing piety and
love of Torah, a life in which (your/his/her/their)
heart's desires for goodness will be fulfilled.

(You may pause and add your own words of blessing here.)

Amen.[2]

For a Place of Miracle

From *Gates of Prayer*

Days pass and the years vanish,
and we walk sightless among miracles.
God, fill our eyes with seeing
and our minds with knowing.

Help us to see,
wherever we gaze,
that the bush burns unconsumed.
And we,
clay touched by God,
will reach out for holiness,
and exclaim in wonder,

"How filled with awe is this place!"

בָּרוּךְ אַתָּה יְיָ אֱלֹהֵינוּ מֶלֶךְ הָעוֹלָם
שֶׁעָשָׂה נִסִּים בַּמָּקוֹם הַזֶּה.

Barukh atah Adonai Eloheinu melekh ha'olam,
she'asah nissim bamakom hazeh.

Blessed is God, who performed miracles in this
place.[3]

For a Place of Study

If You Really Want to Know,
Chaim Nachman Bialik

If you really want to know the well
from which our martyred forebears drew
their strength of soul. . . .

If you really want to know the well
from which our oppressed forebears drew
God's comfort. . . .

If it is your fondest wish to see the breast
on which was poured a people's tears,
its heart- and soul-felt bitterness,
the place where cries broke out and gushed like
water. . . .

If it is your fondest wish to know the
all-compassionate
mother—aged, devoted, faithful—
whose full-embracing love collects her children's tears,
then wipes the eye that shed them,
then blankets her loved ones in the shade of
stretched-out wings,
and rocks them to sleep on her knees. . . .

Tormented brothers and sisters,
If you do not know all this,
then. . . .

Turn to the synagogue, old and weathered.
To this day, you may see there
in the layers of shadowed darkness,
in some tiny corner, or before a wood-burning
stove—
like skinny stocks of wheat, just a specter
of something long since come and gone—
Jews with faces shrunk and wrinkled
Golus *Jews weighed down by exile,*
Who, nonetheless,
Lose their cares
In a tattered page of Talmud

Or the age-old conversations of Midrash,
And wipe out worry by reciting psalms.
How desolate a sight this is to strangers
Who will never understand.
But your heart will tell you
That your feet tread the threshold of our House of
    Life,
Your eyes see the storehouse of our soul.

מוֹדֶה אֲנִי לְפָנֶיךָ יְיָ אֱלֹהַי שֶׁשַּׂמְתָּ חֶלְקִי מִיוֹשְׁבֵי
בֵית הַמִּדְרָשׁ
וְלֹא שַׂמְתָּ חֶלְקִי מִיוֹשְׁבֵי קְרָנוֹת.
שָׁאֲנִי מַשְׁכִּים וְהֵם מַשְׁכִּימִים,
אֲנִי מַשְׁכִּים לְדִבְרֵי תוֹרָה, וְהֵם מַשְׁכִּימִים
לִדְבָרִים בְּטֵלִים

Modeh ani l'fanekha Adonai Elohai, shesamta
    chelki miyoshvei vet hamidrash, vlo samta
    chelki miyoshvei k'ranot.
She'ani mashkim vehem mashkimim.
Ani mashkim l'divrei torah vhem mashkimim
    lid'varim v'telim.

בָּרוּךְ אַתָּה, יְיָ אֱלֹהֵינוּ, מֶלֶךְ הָעוֹלָם,
אֲשֶׁר קִדְּשָׁנוּ בְּמִצְוֹתָיו וְצִוָּנוּ לַעֲסוֹק בְּדִבְרֵי תוֹרָה.

Barukh atah Adonai Eloheinu melekh ha'olam
asher kidshanu b'mitzvotav v'tzivanu la'asok
b'divrei torah.

O my God, I thank you:
for giving me a place among those who sit in the
    house of study,
not among street-corner loiterers.
We both rise together at the break of day.
But I arise to words of Torah, and they arise to
    empty chatter.
Blessed is God, who commands us to study
    Torah.[4]

On Praying in a Synagogue, New or Old

Jewish tradition remembers Balaam, hired by the king of Moab to curse the Israelites. Looking down upon the Jewish camp from a precipice on high, Balaam confessed:

> How can I damn whom God has not damned,
> How doom when Adonai has not doomed?
> Who can count the dust of Jacob,
> Number the dust-cloud of Israel?
> May I die the death of the upright,
> May my fate be like theirs.
> How lovely are your tents O Jacob,
> Your dwellings O Israel.[5]

By the Middle Ages, it became common to repeat an expanded version of Balaam's words when entering a synagogue to pray. Unlike Balaam, who could not count the Jews he saw, we do count ourselves, gathered for a *minyan*, and medieval Jews used the expansion of Balaam's prayer to do it. In the old manuscripts, the second Hebrew line sometimes appears in large type, reminding worshippers that it had exactly ten words. As the *minyan* gathered, its members recited the first line together, then used each of the following ten words to number off those in attendance. Today, the prayer remains with us still, a fitting meditation upon entering a synagogue, and a subtle recollection of God's blessing upon us. In just a few more years, Israel's population will outnumber the Jews of America, making Israel the population center of the Jewish People. "Who can count the dust of Jacob / Number the dust-cloud of Israel?"

When you are in Israel, you will surely want to attend a synagogue, joining your voice of prayer to those of our people who bring together liturgical traditions from the four corners of the earth.

When you go, say the traditional prayer from our Siddur, as follows, letting each of the ten words in the second line remind you of the blessing we enjoy, back home at last in the land of our ancestors.

(While outside the synagogue, say:)

מַה טֹּבוּ אֹהָלֶיךָ יַעֲקֹב,
מִשְׁכְּנֹתֶיךָ יִשְׂרָאֵל.

Mah tovu ohalekha ya'akov,
mishk'notekha Yisrael.

How lovely are your tents, O Jacob, your dwellings O Israel.

(As you walk through the synagogue doorway, say the following sentence, word by word.)

Va'ani	וַאֲנִי
b'rov	בְּרֹב
chasd'kha	חַסְדְּךָ
avo	אָבֹא
veitekha	בֵיתֶךָ,
eshtachaveh	אֶשְׁתַּחֲוֶה
el	אֶל
heikhal	הֵיכַל
kod'sh'kha	קָדְשְׁךָ
b'yiratekha	בְּיִרְאָתֶךָ.

As for me, through your abundant mercy, I enter
your house.
In reverence before You, I bow at your sacred center.[6]

(Find a place to sit, and continue ...)

יְיָ, אָהַבְתִּי מְעוֹן בֵּיתֶךָ, וּמְקוֹם מִשְׁכַּן כְּבוֹדֶךָ.
וַאֲנִי אֶשְׁתַּחֲוֶה וְאֶכְרָעָה, אֶבְרְכָה לִפְנֵי יְיָ עֹשִׂי.
וַאֲנִי תְפִלָּתִי לְךָ, יְיָ, עֵת רָצוֹן;
אֱלֹהִים, בְּרָב חַסְדֶּךָ, עֲנֵנִי בֶּאֱמֶת יִשְׁעֶךָ.

O my God, I love your abode, the place where
your glory dwells.
I will bow and bend my knees, giving praise to
God, my maker.
Adonai, I offer You my prayer, at this fitting time.
God, in your abundant kindness, answer me with
your saving truth.

For a Place of Recent Tragedy

Every book should have a page it will not need
   some day,
Perforated at the margin for easy disposal,
Like a tear-off ticket to the world to come,
Or raffle chances you buy from scouts, local school
   boards, or the Heart Association,
Only this time, you get to win, not just save the
   stub in last year's files of things that never hap-
   pened.
When Elijah comes, he gets the page,
Testimony to the time that you put in, waiting,
When messianic hopes seemed dashed with every
   passing headline.
You were there.

Maybe the page is like those tickets that you used
   to buy
For trains that picked up passengers at every tiny
   crossing,
And you measured how far you had come by the
   number of punchholes
That your ticket had collected,
One for each unwanted stop along the way.
My Jewish ticket would be practically in shambles
   now,
So many punches through the years: Babi Yar,
   Terezin, the Munich Olympics. . . .
Elijah takes the ticket gently, folds it away at last,
   and says, You're finally home.
But keep the stub of course, to remember the train
   ride.
You were there.

This is the page my book would rather do without,
Punch-marked and perforated for past and future.
We pilgrim through time in the hope that our train
   will not stop
At yet another crossing where we'd rather not get
   out,
Praying that the page will soon be claimed at the
   end of the ride.

Or at least that the hardest part of the journey is
  over—
We'll skip over the page, no need to stop to have it
  punched again.
But if, perchance, there are a few more destinations
  to our destiny
Crossroads in time where once again
    some blood is spilled
    some laughter stilled,
    a single breath of life, needlessly cut off,
This page remains for somber presentation on the
  spot,
That you might know:
You were there.

יִתְגַּדַּל וְיִתְקַדַּשׁ שְׁמֵהּ רַבָּא

Yit-ga-dal v'yit-ka-dash sh'meih rabba

Mayence, Blois, York

בְּעָלְמָא דִּי בְרָא כִרְעוּתֵהּ
וְיַמְלִיךְ מַלְכוּתֵהּ

b'al'ma di-vra khi-ru-tei v'yam-likh mal-khu-tei

Dachau, Buchenwald, Babi Yar

בְּחַיֵּיכוֹן וּבְיוֹמֵיכוֹן וּבְחַיֵּי דְכָל בֵּית יִשְׂרָאֵל
בַּעֲגָלָא וּבִזְמַן קָרִיב וְאִמְרוּ אָמֵן.

b'cha-yei-khon uv'yo-mei-khon
uv'cha-yei d'khol beit Yisrael
Ba'a-ga-la u-viz-man ka-riv v'im-ru amen!

Kishinev, Warsaw, Auschwitz

יְהֵא שְׁמֵהּ רַבָּא מְבָרַךְ לְעָלַם וּלְעָלְמֵי עָלְמַיָּא.
יִתְבָּרַךְ וְיִשְׁתַּבַּח וְיִתְפָּאַר וְיִתְרוֹמַם
וְיִתְנַשֵּׂא וְיִתְהַדָּר וְיִתְעַלֶּה וְיִתְהַלָּל
שְׁמֵהּ דְּקֻדְשָׁא בְּרִיךְ הוּא

Yehei shmeih rabba m'va-rakh
l'a-lam ul'al-mei al-maya
yit-ba-rakh v'yish-ta-bach v'yit-pa'ar

v'yit-ro-mam v'yit-na-sei
v'yit-ha-dar v'yit-a-leh v'yit-ha-lal
sh'meih d'kud-sha b'rikh hu

Treblinka, Chelmno, Bergen-Belsen

לְעֵלָּא מִן כָּל בִּרְכָתָא וְשִׁירָתָא
תֻּשְׁבְּחָתָא וְנֶחֱמָתָא דַּאֲמִירָן בְּעָלְמָא
וְאִמְרוּ אָמֵן.

L'ei-la min kol bir-kha-ta v'shi-ra-ta
tush-b'cha-ta v'ne-che-ma-ta
da'a-mi-ran b'al-ma
v'im-ru amen!

K'far Etzion, Munich, Ma'alot
Machaneh Yehudah, Ben Yehudah Street

יְהֵא שְׁלָמָא רַבָּא מִן שְׁמַיָּא
וְחַיִּים עָלֵינוּ וְעַל כָּל יִשְׂרָאֵל
וְאִמְרוּ אָמֵן.

Y'hei sh'lama rabba min sh'maya
v'cha-yim aleinu v'al kol yisrael
v'im-ru amen

(Add name of recent tragedy here)

עֹשֶׂה שָׁלוֹם בִּמְרוֹמָיו
הוּא יַעֲשֶׂה שָׁלוֹם עָלֵינוּ וְעַל כָּל יִשְׂרָאֵל
וְאִמְרוּ אָמֵן.

O-seh shalom bim-ro-mav hu ya'aseh shalom
alenu v'al kol yisrael, v'im-ru amen[7]

*Let the glory of God be extolled, let God's great
name be hallowed, in the world whose creation
God willed. May God's dominion soon prevail,
in our own day, our own lives, and the life of all
Israel, and let us say: Amen.*
Let God's great name be blessed for ever and ever.
*Let the name of Holy Blessed One be glorified, ex-
alted, and honored, though God is beyond all the
praises, songs, and adorations that we can utter,
and let us say: Amen.*

*For us and for all Israel, may the blessing of peace
and the promise of life come true, and let us say:
Amen.*

*May the One who causes peace to reign in the high
heavens let peace descend on us, and on all Israel,
and let us say: Amen.* [8]

For a Place of Wisdom

Rabbi Yose Ben Kisma said:

Once, when I was walking along the way, I
chanced upon a man who exchanged greetings
with me. "Rabbi," he asked, "Where are you from?"

"From a large city of scholars and sages," I replied.

"Would you care to dwell with us, Rabbi?" he
inquired. "I will make you a millionaire in gifts of
cash and precious gems."

I responded, "Young man, were you to give me
all the silver, gold, cash, and jewels in the entire
world, I would never dwell anywhere but where
there is Torah. When you die, you will be accompanied
not by silver, gold, and precious stones but by
Torah and good deeds alone, as it is written, 'It shall
guide you when you walk, watch over you when
you lie down, and be your subject for discussion,
when you wake up' (Proverbs 6:22). 'It shall guide
you when you walk,' in this world; it will 'watch
over you when you lie down' in the grave; 'and be
your subject for discussion, when you wake up'—in
the world to come."

בָּרוּךְ אַתָּה, יְיָ אֱלֹהֵינוּ, מֶלֶךְ הָעוֹלָם,
שֶׁחָלַק מֵחָכְמָתוֹ לִירֵאָיו.

*Barukh atah Adonai Eloheinu melekh ha'olam
shechalak meichokhmato li'rei'av.*

Blessed is God, who shares divine wisdom with
those who are God-fearing. [9]

For a Place of War

Lament, Yehuda Amichai

The diameter of the bomb was thirty centimeters
  and the diameter of its destruction—
    about seven meters,
      and in it, four killed and eleven wounded.
        and around these, in a larger circle
          of pain and time, are scattered
            two hospitals and one cemetery,
              But the young woman
                who was buried in the place
                  from where she came, at a distance
                    of more than one hundred kilometers,
                      enlarges the circle considerably,
                        And the lonely man
                          who is mourning her death in a distant country
                            incorporates into the circle
                              the whole world. And I won't speak
                                of the cry of the orphans
                                  that reaches God's chair and from there
                                    makes the circle endless
                                      and godless.

אֲנִי מַבְטִיחַ לָךְ,
יַלְדָּה שֶׁלִי קְטַנָּה,
שֶׁזּוֹ תִּהְיֶה
הַמִּלְחָמָה הָאַחֲרוֹנָה.

Ani mavtiach lakh
yaldah sheli k'tanah
shezo
tihyeh
hamilchamah ha'acharonah.

I promise you my child,
I vow with all my might,
That this will be the last,
The final war that we will fight.

בָּרוּךְ אַתָּה יְיָ אֱלֹהֵינוּ מֶלֶךְ הָעוֹלָם עשֶׁה הַשָּׁלוֹם.

Barukh atah Adonai Eloheinu melekh ha'olam,
oseh hashalom.

Blessed is God, who will bring peace.

For a Place of Hope

Hatikvah (The national anthem of Israel)

כָּל עוֹד בַּלֵּבָב פְּנִימָה
נֶפֶשׁ יְהוּדִי הוֹמִיָּה,
וּלְפַאֲתֵי מִזְרָח קָדִימָה
עַיִן לְצִיּוֹן צוֹפִיָּה,
עוֹד לֹא אָבְדָה תִקְוָתֵנוּ
הַתִּקְוָה בַּת שְׁנוֹת אַלְפַּיִם,
לִהְיוֹת עַם חָפְשִׁי בְּאַרְצֵנוּ,
בְּאֶרֶץ צִיּוֹן וִירוּשָׁלַיִם.

Kol od baleivav p'nimah
Nefesh y'hudi homiyah
Ul'fa'atei mizrach kadimah
Ayin l'tsiyon tsofiyah

Od lo av'da tikvateinu
Hatikvah bat shnot alpayim
Lihyot am chofshi b'artzeinu
B'eretz tsiyon viyerushalayim

(Repeat last four lines)

As long as deep in the heart
A Jewish soul yearns,
And toward the East,
An eye looks to Zion,

Our hope is not yet lost—
The hope of 2,000 years:
To be a free people in our land,
The land of Zion and Jerusalem.[10]

בָּרוּךְ אַתָּה יְיָ מִקְוֵה יִשְׂרָאֵל.

Barukh atah Adonai, mikveh Yisrael.[11]

Blessed is God, the hope of Israel.

For a Place of Muslim or Christian Worship

Maimonides, Code of Jewish Law

Adam, the first man, was assigned six commandments: not to worship idols, not to take God's name
in vain, not to murder, not to engage in forbidden
sexual relations, not to steal, and to maintain courts
to see that justice based on these laws was upheld.
When Noah came along, a further commandment
was given to non-Jews: not to eat meat torn from a
living animal. All in all, then, God's covenant with
non-Jews encompasses seven laws.

The Talmud

Our Rabbis taught: we support the poor who are
not Jewish along with those who are; we visit the
sick who are not Jewish just as we do Jews; we
bury the deceased who are not Jewish just as we
do Jews—*mipnei darkhei shalom*—in the interests
of peace.

בָּרוּךְ אַתָּה יְיָ הַמַּדְרִיכֵנוּ בְּדַרְכֵי שָׁלוֹם.

*Barukh atah Adonai, hamadrikheinu b'darkhei
shalom.*

Blessed is God who sets our steps in the ways of
peace.[12]

For Seeing or Hearing Hebrew All around You

Hebrew, Danny Siegel

I'll tell you how much I love Hebrew:
Read me anything—
Genesis

or an ad in an Israeli paper
and watch my face.
I will make half-sounds of ecstasy
and my smile will be so enormously sweet
you would think some angels were singing Psalms
  or God Himself was reciting to me.
I am crazy for her Holiness
  and each restaurant's menu in Yerushalayim
  or Bialik poem
gives me peace no Dante or Milton or Goethe
could give.
I have heard Iliads of poetry,
Omar Khayyam in Farsi,
and Virgil sung as if the poet himself
were coaching the reader.
And they move me—
but not like
the train schedule from Haifa to Tel Aviv
or the choppy unsyntaxed note
from a student who got half the grammar I taught
  him
all wrong
but remembered to write with Alefs and Zayins and
  Shins.
That's the way I am.
I'd rather hear the weather report
on Kol Yisrael
than all the rhythms and music of Shakespeare.

For Planting a Tree

Before picking up the sapling, say:

Rabbi Yochanan ben Zakkai used to say: If you are
holding a sapling in your hands, and someone an-
nounces the Messiah's arrival, plant the sapling, and
after that, go meet the Messiah. [13]

The Tree and the Mashiach (the Messiah),
Danny Siegel

No matter what reasonable people
or foaming enthusiastic youths tell you:
that this messiah or that messiah
is imminent—
plant!
The *Mashiach* is in no rush.
When you have planted down the last clods of dirt,
And watered your pines, your cedars,
your gum trees and cypresses,
he will still be wherever he is supposed to be,
and more than happy to admire the sapling with
    you.
Messiahs don't come to uproot things. . . .

Pick up the sapling and, while holding it in your hand, say:

*As my ancestors planted for me, I now plant for my
   descendants:*[14]

בָּרוּךְ אַתָּה יְיָ אֱלֹהֵינוּ מֶלֶךְ הָעוֹלָם
מַצְמִיחַ כָּל עֵץ חַיִּים.

*Barukh atah Adonai Eloheinu melekh ha'olam
matzmi'ach kol eits chayim.*

Blessed is God, who raises up each tree of life.[15]

On Eating at a Kibbutz

You may have a chance either to eat a meal in a kibbutz or
to walk through the fields and orchards and pick some fruit
or produce. Tradition sees special merit in food grown in
the land of Israel, and we should, too, especially given the
modern miracle of making what was just desert or swampland blossom. The Rabbis provided special blessings for the
occasion.

Upon picking fresh fruit or garden produce, say:

כַּמָּה נָאָה תְּנוּבַת הַשָּׂדֶה זוֹ ____ .
בָּרוּךְ הַמָּקוֹם שֶׁבְּרָאָהּ.

Kamah na'ah t'nuvat hasadeh zo _____ .
Barukh hamakom sheb'ra'ah.

How good is this (name of food).
Blessed is God who created it.[16]

Before eating add:

For fruit that grows on trees . . .

בָּרוּךְ אַתָּה יְיָ אֱלֹהֵינוּ מֶלֶךְ הָעוֹלָם בּוֹרֵא פְּרִי הָעֵץ.

Barukh atah Adonai Eloheinu melekh ha'olam,
borei p'ri ha'etz.

Blessed is God, for creating fruit of the trees.

For produce that grows from the soil . . .

בָּרוּךְ אַתָּה יְיָ אֱלֹהֵינוּ מֶלֶךְ הָעוֹלָם
בּוֹרֵא פְּרִי הָאֲדָמָה.

Barukh atah Adonai Eloheinu melekh ha'olam,
borei p'ri ha'adamah.

Blessed is God, for creating produce from the earth.

Upon eating cake or pastry made from grain grown in Eretz Yisrael, *say:*

בָּרוּךְ אַתָּה יְיָ אֱלֹהֵינוּ מֶלֶךְ הָעוֹלָם
בּוֹרֵא מִינֵי מְזוֹנוֹת.

Barukh atah Adonai Eloheinu melekh ha'olam,
borei minei m'zonot.

Blessed is God for creating varieties of grain.

Upon eating a meal at the kibbutz, say:

בָּרוּךְ אַתָּה יְיָ אֱלֹהֵינוּ מֶלֶךְ הָעוֹלָם
אֲשֶׁר בָּרָא מַעֲדַנִּים לְעַדֵּן בָּהֶם נֶפֶשׁ כָּל חַי.
בָּרוּךְ אַתָּה יְיָ עַל הָאָרֶץ וְעַל מַעֲדַנֶּיהָ.

Barukh atah Adonai Eloheinu melekh ha'olam,
asher bara ma'adanim l'aden bahem nefesh
kol chai.
Barukh atah Adonai, al ha'aretz v'al
ma'adaneha.

Blessed is God for creating delightful food to give
pleasure to living creatures.
Blessed is God for the land and its delights.[17]

Before eating bread, add:

How good is this bread. Blessed is God who created it.[18]

בָּרוּךְ אַתָּה יְיָ אֱלֹהֵינוּ מֶלֶךְ הָעוֹלָם
הַמּוֹצִיא לֶחֶם מִן הָאָרֶץ.

Barukh atah Adonai Eloheinu melekh ha'olam,
hamotsi lechem min ha'aretz.

Blessed is God, for bringing forth bread from the
earth.

After eating, say the following:

בָּרוּךְ אַתָּה, יְיָ אֱלֹהֵינוּ, מֶלֶךְ הָעוֹלָם, עַל הַגֶּפֶן
וְעַל פְּרִי הַגֶּפֶן, וְעַל תְּנוּבַת הַשָּׂדֶה, וְעַל אֶרֶץ
חֶמְדָּה טוֹבָה וּרְחָבָה שֶׁרָצִיתָ וְהִנְחַלְתָּ לַאֲבוֹתֵינוּ
לֶאֱכֹל מִפִּרְיָהּ וְלִשְׂבֹּעַ מִטּוּבָהּ. רַחֶם-נָא, יְיָ אֱלֹהֵינוּ,
עַל יִשְׂרָאֵל עַמֶּךָ, וְעַל יְרוּשָׁלַיִם עִירֶךָ, וְעַל צִיּוֹן
מִשְׁכַּן כְּבוֹדֶךָ. וּבְנֵה יְרוּשָׁלַיִם עִיר הַקֹּדֶשׁ בִּמְהֵרָה
בְיָמֵינוּ, וְהַעֲלֵנוּ לְתוֹכָהּ וְשַׂמְּחֵנוּ בְּבִנְיָנָהּ, וְנֹאכַל
מִפִּרְיָהּ וְנִשְׂבַּע מִטּוּבָהּ, וּנְבָרֶכְךָ עָלֶיהָ בִּקְדֻשָּׁה
וּבְטָהֳרָה. כִּי אַתָּה, יְיָ, טוֹב וּמֵטִיב לַכֹּל, וְנוֹדֶה לְךָ
עַל הָאָרֶץ וְעַל פְּרִי הַגֶּפֶן. בָּרוּךְ אַתָּה, יְיָ, עַל הָאָרֶץ
וְעַל פְּרִי הַגֶּפֶן.

Blessed is God for the fruit of the vine and the produce of the field, for the lovely and spacious land that you gave to our ancestors, as a heritage from which to eat the produce and to be satisfied by its goodness. Have mercy, Eternal our God, on Israel your people, on Jerusalem your city, and on Zion, the abode of your glory. Rebuild the holy city of Jerusalem speedily and in our days. Bring us there and gladden us with its revival. May we eat of the fruit of the Land and enjoy its good-ness—for which we praise you in holiness and purity. Because you are good and render good to all, we acknowledge you for the Land and for its produce.

בָּרוּךְ אַתָּה יְיָ הַטּוֹב וְהַמֵּטִיב.

Barukh atah Adonai hatov vehameitiv.

Blessed is God, who is good and does good.[19]

For a Variety of Special Occasions

Israel is a land where our blessings were first formulated—and no wonder: there is so much that takes the breath away. The following list of blessings reflects the everyday wonders you may encounter. All the blessings are traditional, either taken directly from the *Siddur* or borrowed from rabbinic literature.

On seeing a friend or relative whom you have not seen for over 30 days:

בָּרוּךְ אַתָּה יְיָ אֱלֹהֵינוּ מֶלֶךְ הָעוֹלָם
שֶׁהֶחֱיָנוּ וְקִיְּמָנוּ וְהִגִּיעָנוּ לַזְּמַן הַזֶּה.

Barukh atah Adonai Eloheinu melekh ha'olam, shehecheyanu v'ki'manu v'higiyanu laz'man hazeh.

Blessed is God who has kept us in life, sustained us and brought us to this moment.

On seeing a friend or relative whom you have not seen for over a year:

בָּרוּךְ אַתָּה יְיָ אֱלֹהֵינוּ מֶלֶךְ הָעוֹלָם מְחַיֵּה הַמֵּתִים.

Barukh atah Adonai Eloheinu melekh ha'olam, m'chayeh hameitim.

Blessed is God, who revives the dead.

On seeing the wonders of nature: deserts, valleys, mountains, whatever moves you:

בָּרוּךְ אַתָּה יְיָ אֱלֹהֵינוּ מֶלֶךְ הָעוֹלָם
עֹשֶׂה מַעֲשֶׂה בְרֵאשִׁית.

Barukh atah Adonai Eloheinu melekh ha'olam, oseh ma'aseh v'reishit.

Blessed is God, who shaped the work of creation.

On seeing rain:

בָּרוּךְ אַתָּה יְיָ אֱלֹהֵינוּ מֶלֶךְ הָעוֹלָם הַטּוֹב וְהַמֵּטִיב.

Barukh atah Adonai Eloheinu melekh ha'olam, hatov vehameitiv.

Blessed is God who is good and does good.

On seeing a rainbow:

בָּרוּךְ אַתָּה יְיָ, אֱלֹהֵינוּ מֶלֶךְ הָעוֹלָם, זוֹכֵר הַבְּרִית
וְנֶאֱמָן בִּבְרִיתוֹ וְקַיָּם בְּמַאֲמָרוֹ.

Barukh atah Adonai Eloheinu melekh ha'olam zokher habreet, v'ne'eman bivreeto v'kayam b'ma'amaro.

Blessed is God who remembers the covenant, who is faithful to the covenant, and whose word stands firm.

On hearing thunder, seeing lightning, or experiencing a violent windstorm:

בָּרוּךְ אַתָּה יְיָ, אֱלֹהֵינוּ מֶלֶךְ הָעוֹלָם,
שֶׁכֹּחוֹ וּגְבוּרָתוֹ מָלֵא עוֹלָם.

*Barukh atah Adonai Eloheinu melekh ha'olam,
shekocho ug'vurato malei olam.*

Blessed is God whose might and power fill the
universe.

On seeing blossoming trees or shrubs:

בָּרוּךְ אַתָּה יְיָ, אֱלֹהֵינוּ מֶלֶךְ הָעוֹלָם,
שֶׁלֹּא חִסַּר בְּעוֹלָמוֹ דָּבָר
וּבָרָא בּוֹ בְּרִיּוֹת טוֹבוֹת וְאִילָנוֹת טוֹבִים
לְהַנּוֹת בָּהֶם בְּנֵי אָדָם.

*Barukh atah Adonai Eloheinu melekh ha'olam,
shelo chisar b'olamo davar uvara vo v'riyot
tovot v'ilanot tovim l'hanot bahem b'nei adam.*

Blessed is God whose universe lacks absolutely
nothing, who has created it with beautiful creatures and lovely trees so that human beings may
enjoy them.

On seeing the new moon:

בָּרוּךְ אַתָּה יְיָ אֱלֹהֵינוּ מֶלֶךְ הָעוֹלָם
מְחַדֵּשׁ רָאשֵׁי חֳדָשִׁים.

*Barukh atah Adonai Eloheinu melekh ha'olam,
m'chadesh roshei chodashim.*

Blessed is God, who renews the moon.

*On observing evidence of the love of the land among the
people who live there:*

בָּרוּךְ אַתָּה יְיָ אֱלֹהֵינוּ מֶלֶךְ הָעוֹלָם
שֶׁנָּתַן חֵן מָקוֹם עַל יוֹשְׁבָיו.

*Barukh atah Adonai Eloheinu melekh ha'olam,
shenatan chen makom al yoshvav.*

Blessed is God, who inspires the inhabitants of a place with love for where they dwell.

On observing archaeological remains of pagan worship:

בָּרוּךְ אַתָּה יְיָ אֱלֹהֵינוּ מֶלֶךְ הָעוֹלָם
שֶׁעָקַר עֲבוֹדָה זָרָה מֵאַרְצֵנוּ.

*Barukh atah Adonai Eloheinu melekh ha'olam,
she'akar avodah zarah me'artseinu.*

Blessed is God, who has uprooted idolatry from our land.

On seeing new homes for people who have resettled Israel's wasteland:

בָּרוּךְ אַתָּה יְיָ אֱלֹהֵינוּ מֶלֶךְ הָעוֹלָם
מַצִּיב גְּבוּל אַלְמָנָה.

*Barukh atah Adonai Eloheinu melekh ha'olam,
matsiv g'vul almanah.*

Blessed is God, who establishes landmarks for the widowed country.

For the Airplane: Prayer for a Safe Journey to Israel

מִי שֶׁבֵּרַךְ אֲבוֹתֵינוּ,
אַבְרָהָם יִצְחָק וְיַעֲקֹב,
שָׂרָה, רִבְקָה, רָחֵל וְלֵאָה,
יְבָרְכֵנִי
וְאֶת הַנּוֹסְעִים אִתִּי
בְּזוּ נְסִיעָתֵנוּ לְאֶרֶץ יִשְׂרָאֵל.
יְהִי רָצוֹן מִלְּפָנֶיךָ
שֶׁנִּסַּע לְשָׁלוֹם,
וְשֶׁנַּגִּיעַ בְּשָׁלוֹם לְאֶרֶץ חֶמְדַּת לִבֵּינוּ,

לְאֶרֶץ צִיּוֹן.
יְהִי רָצוֹן מִלְּפָנֶיךָ שֶׁנַּחֲזֹר
מְבֹרָכִים בְּכָל מַעֲשֵׂינוּ,
מְחֻדָּשִׁים מֵעַמֵּנוּ בִּמְדִינָתֵנוּ.

God of our fathers and mothers,
Set us on our journey and guide us
that we may reach our destination joyously alive
    and at peace.
Deliver us from all danger on the way.
May we merit favor, kindness, and compassion in
    your sight,
and in the sight of all who see us.
Blessed are You, God, for hearing prayer.[20]

May the One who blessed our ancestors,
Abraham, Isaac and Jacob, Sarah, Rebekah, Rachel
    and Leah,
Bless me, _____ , and those who travel with me,
As we leave for the land of Israel.
May we travel there safely,
And arrive in peace to the land we hold dear,
the land we call Zion.
May we return, blessed in every undertaking,
Inspired and renewed by our people in our land.

Meditation for Traveling to Israel: Am I a Tourist or a Pilgrim?

Tourists, by Yehuda Amichai

Visits of condolence is all we get from them.
They squat at the Holocaust Memorial,
They put on grave faces at the Wailing Wall
And they laugh behind heavy curtains
In their hotels.
They have their pictures taken
Together with our famous dead
At Rachel's Tomb and Herzl's tomb
And on the top of Ammunition Hill.
They weep over our sweet boys
And lust over our tough girls

And hang up their underwear
To dry quickly
in cool, blue bathrooms.

Once I sat on the steps by a gate at David's
Tower. I placed my two heavy baskets at my side.
A group of tourists was standing around their guide
and I became their target marker.
"You see that man with the baskets? Just right
of his head there's an arch from the Roman period.
Just right of his head."
"But he's moving, he's moving!" I said to myself:
Redemption will come only if their guide tells them,
"You see that arch from the Roman period? It's not
important: but next to it, left and down a bit, there
sits a man who's bought fruit and vegetables for his
family."

For the Airplane: Prayer for a Safe Journey Home

יְהִי רָצוֹן מִלְּפָנֶיךָ, יְיָ אֱלֹהֵינוּ וֵאלֹהֵי אֲבוֹתֵינוּ,
שֶׁתּוֹלִיכֵנוּ לְשָׁלוֹם וְתַצְעִידֵנוּ לְשָׁלוֹם,
וְתַגִּיעֵנוּ אֶל מְחוֹז חֶפְצֵנוּ לְחַיִּים וּלְשִׂמְחָה וּלְשָׁלוֹם.
וְתַצִּילֵנוּ מִכַּף כָּל אוֹיֵב וְאוֹרֵב וְאָסוֹן בַּדֶּרֶךְ,
וְתִתְּנֵנוּ לְחֵן וּלְחֶסֶד וּלְרַחֲמִים
בְּעֵינֶיךָ וּבְעֵינֵי כָל רוֹאֵינוּ.
וְתִשְׁמַע קוֹל תַּחֲנוּנֵינוּ,
כִּי אֵל שׁוֹמֵעַ תְּפִלָּה וְתַחֲנוּן אָתָּה.
בָּרוּךְ אַתָּה, יְיָ, שׁוֹמֵעַ תְּפִלָּה.

God of our fathers and mothers,
Set us on our journey and guide us
that we may reach our destination joyously alive
    and at peace.
Deliver us from all danger on the way.
May we merit favor, kindness, and compassion in
    your sight,
and in the sight of all who see us.
Blessed are You, God, for hearing prayer.[21]

On Waking Up and Going to Bed Each Day

On Waking Up

בָּרוּךְ אַתָּה יְיָ אֱלֹהֵינוּ מֶלֶךְ הָעוֹלָם,
אֲשֶׁר יָצַר אֶת הָאָדָם בְּחָכְמָה,
וּבָרָא בוֹ נְקָבִים נְקָבִים, חֲלוּלִים חֲלוּלִים.
גָּלוּי וְיָדוּעַ לִפְנֵי כִסֵּא כְבוֹדֶךָ,
שֶׁאִם יִפָּתֵחַ אֶחָד מֵהֶם אוֹ יִסָּתֵם אֶחָד מֵהֶם
אִי אֶפְשָׁר לְהִתְקַיֵּם וְלַעֲמוֹד לְפָנֶיךָ.
בָּרוּךְ אַתָּה, יְיָ, רוֹפֵא כָל בָּשָׂר וּמַפְלִיא לַעֲשׂוֹת.

We praise You, God,
for shaping humankind with wisdom,
for creating in us ducts and organs,
knowing well
that if this one opens or that one closes
our life on earth would end.
Blessed is God, whose work is marvelous.

אֱלֹהַי, נְשָׁמָה שֶׁנָּתַתָּ בִּי טְהוֹרָה הִיא.
אַתָּה בְרָאתָהּ, אַתָּה יְצַרְתָּהּ, אַתָּה נְפַחְתָּהּ בִּי,
וְאַתָּה מְשַׁמְּרָהּ בְּקִרְבִּי, וְאַתָּה עָתִיד לִטְּלָהּ מִמֶּנִּי
וּלְהַחֲזִירָהּ בִּי לֶעָתִיד לָבֹא.
כָּל זְמַן שֶׁהַנְּשָׁמָה בְקִרְבִּי מוֹדֶה אֲנִי לְפָנֶיךָ,
יְיָ אֱלֹהַי וֵאלֹהֵי אֲבוֹתַי, רִבּוֹן כָּל הַמַּעֲשִׂים,
אֲדוֹן כָּל הַנְּשָׁמוֹת.
בָּרוּךְ אַתָּה, יְיָ, הַמַּחֲזִיר נְשָׁמוֹת לִפְגָרִים מֵתִים.

My God, the soul You gave is pure.
You created it, shaped it, breathed it into me.
You care for it within me,
will some day take it from me,
and return it to me in a time to come.
As long as I have my soul, I will acknowledge You,
my God and God of those who came before me,
Master of material being and of the soul.
Blessed is God who restores souls to the dead.

מוֹדֶה אֲנִי לְפָנֶיךָ, מֶלֶךְ חַי וְקַיָּם, שֶׁהֶחֱזַרְתָּ בִּי
נִשְׁמָתִי בְּחֶמְלָה; רַבָּה אֱמוּנָתֶךָ.

224

Modeh ani l'fanekha melekh chai v'kayam
shehechezarta bi nishmati b'chemlah rabbah
emunatekhah.

I give thanks to You, Eternal One,
For restoring my soul. Great is your faithfulness.[22]

On Going to Bed

יְהִי רָצוֹן מִלְּפָנֶיךָ יְיָ אֱלֹהַי שֶׁתַּשְׁכִּיבֵנִי לְשָׁלוֹם
וְתֵן חֶלְקִי בְּתוֹרָתֶךָ
וְתַרְגִּילֵנִי לִידֵי מִצְוָה
וְאַל תַּרְגִּילֵנִי לִידֵי עֲבֵירָה
וְאַל תְּבִיאֵנִי לִידֵי חֵטְא וְלֹא לִידֵי עָוֹן וְלֹא לִידֵי
נִסָּיוֹן וְלֹא לִידֵי בִזָּיוֹן
וְיִשְׁלוֹט בִּי יֵצֶר טוֹב וְאַל יִשְׁלוֹט בִּי יֵצֶר הָרָע
וְתַצִּילֵנִי מִפֶּגַע רָע וּמֵחֳלָאִים רָעִים
וְאַל יְבַהֲלוּנִי חֲלוֹמוֹת רָעִים וְהִרְהוּרִים רָעִים
וּתְהֵא מִטָּתִי שְׁלֵמָה לְפָנֶיךָ
וְהָאֵר עֵינַי פֶּן אִישַׁן הַמָּוֶת
בָּרוּךְ אַתָּה יְיָ הַמֵּאִיר לָעוֹלָם כּוּלוֹ בִּכְבוֹדוֹ.
בְּיָדוֹ אַפְקִיד רוּחִי בְּעֵת אִישַׁן וְאָעִירָה.
וְעִם רוּחִי גְּוִיָּתִי יְיָ לִי וְלֹא אִירָא.

My God, lie me down in peace
and grant me a portion in your Torah.
Accustom me to mitzvot—
to doing good not evil.
Deliver me from sin and wrong,
from temptation and shame.
Let my inclination for good, not evil, reign me in.
Save me from mishap and disease;
let nightmares and nighttime thoughts not
overwhelm me.
Let me sleep peacefully in your presence.
Wake me up, lest I sleep the sleep of the dead.
Blessed is God, who awakens the world with glory.
Asleep or awake, I leave my soul in God's hands.
And with my soul, my body too.
God is with me; I do not fear.[23]

בָּרוּךְ אַתָּה יְיָ אֱלֹהֵינוּ מֶלֶךְ הָעוֹלָם
אֲשֶׁר קִדְּשָׁנוּ בְּמִצְוֹתָיו
וְצִוָּנוּ לְהַמְלִיכוֹ בְּלֵבָב שָׁלֵם,
וּלְיַחֲדוֹ בְלֵב טוֹב,
וּלְעָבְדוֹ בְּנֶפֶשׁ חֲפֵצָה.

Barukh atah Adonai Eloheinu melekh ha'olam,
asher kidshanu b'mitzvotav
v'tsivanu l'hamlikho b'levav shalem
ul'yachado v'lev tov
ul'ovdo v'nefesh chafetsah

Blessed is God,
who has sanctified us with commandments
and commanded us to recite the Sh'ma
to declare God's royalty with full intention,
to declare God's unity with good intent,
and to serve our God wholeheartedly.
Amen."[24]

שְׁמַע יִשְׂרָאֵל, יְיָ אֱלֹהֵינוּ, יְיָ אֶחָד.

Sh'ma Yisrael Adonai Eloheinu Adonai Echad.

Hear O Israel, Adonai is our God, Adonai alone.

A Meal
in Jerusalem

—————— or ——————

How to Celebrate Like a Pilgrim

For Adonai your God brings you into a good
land, a land of brooks of water, of fountains
and depths that spring out of valleys and
hills; a land of wheat, and barley, and vines,
and fig trees, and pomegranates; a land of
olive oil, and honey; a land where you shall
eat bread without scarceness, you shall not
lack any thing in it; a land whose stones are
iron, and out of whose hills you may dig
bronze. When you have eaten and are full,
then you shall bless Adonai your God for
the good land which was given to you.

—Deuteronomy 8:7–10

Before Eating

Psalm 126

שִׁיר הַמַּעֲלוֹת,
בְּשׁוּב יְיָ אֶת שִׁיבַת צִיּוֹן
הָיִינוּ כְּחֹלְמִים.
אָז יִמָּלֵא שְׂחוֹק פִּינוּ
וּלְשׁוֹנֵנוּ רִנָּה,
אָז יֹאמְרוּ בַגּוֹיִם
הִגְדִּיל יְיָ לַעֲשׂוֹת עִם אֵלֶּה.
הִגְדִּיל יְיָ לַעֲשׂוֹת עִמָּנוּ
הָיִינוּ שְׂמֵחִים.

Shir hama'alot
B'shuv Adonai et shivat tsiyon
hayinu k'cholmim
Az yimalei s'chok pinu
Ul'shoneinu rinah
Az yomru vagoyim
Higdil Adonai la'asot im eleh
Higdil Adonai la'asot imanu
Hayinu s'meikhim

When our God brought back those who returned
to Zion,
We were like dreamers.
Our mouths were filled with laughter
Our tongues with shouts of joy.
Among the nations, people said,
"Adonai has done great things for these people."

Our God has done great things with us,
   and we rejoice.

בָּרוּךְ אַתָּה יְיָ אֱלֹהֵינוּ מֶלֶךְ הָעוֹלָם
הַמּוֹצִיא לֶחֶם מִן הָאָרֶץ.

*Barukh atah Adonai Eloheinu melekh ha'olam,
hamotsi lechem min ha'aretz.*

Blessed is God, who brings forth bread from the
earth.

After Eating

To Redeem the Past
To Celebrate the Present
To Build the Future
A *Birkat Hamazon* from then to now.[1]

*These prayers we are about to say have not been
said for over 1,000 years.*

*Written by our people, here in our land, they
were recited for centuries, but died when our people
were chased from the land in the First Crusade
1,000 years ago. Recovered now, they are ours
again.*

*We make them our own in common identity with
our people through time, from the earliest expression of their hopes to the present rebirth of the land
where those hopes were born.*

*We resurrect these prayers from the dust of centu-
ries, just as we have resurrected the dust itself to be
reborn as modern Israel.*

INVITATION

(Leader:)

בִּרְשׁוּת רַבּוֹתַי, נְבָרֵךְ שֶׁאָכַלְנוּ מִשֶּׁלּוֹ.

Let us praise God of whose food we have eaten.

(Gathering:)

בָּרוּךְ שֶׁאָכַלְנוּ מִשֶּׁלּוֹ וּבְטוּבוֹ חָיִינוּ.

Praised be our God whose food we have eaten
and by whose goodness we live.

BLESSING OF SUSTENANCE

(All:)

בָּרוּךְ אַתָּה, יְיָ, אֱלֹהֵינוּ מֶלֶךְ הָעוֹלָם,
הַזָּנֵינוּ וְלֹא מִמַּעֲשֵׂינוּ,
הַמְפַרְנְסֵינוּ וְלֹא מִצְדְקוֹתֵינוּ.
הַמַּעֲדִיף טוּבוֹ הַגָּדוֹל עָלֵינוּ, כָּאָמוּר:
"פּוֹתֵחַ אֶת יָדֶךָ וּמַשְׂבִּיעַ לְכָל חַי רָצוֹן."
מִטּוּבְךָ תַּשְׂבִּיעֵנוּ
כִּי אַתָּה יוֹצְרֵנוּ.
בָּרוּךְ אַתָּה, יְיָ, הַזָּן אֶת הַכֹּל.

Blessed are You, Adonai, our God, ruler of the
   universe,
For feeding us beyond the measure of our deeds,
And sustaining us beyond what we are worth.
You give us bountifully of your great goodness,
As it is written (Psalm 145:16):
   "You open your hand,
   satisfying the desire of every living thing."
Blessed are You, Adonai, for feeding all.

BLESSING OF THE LAND OF ISRAEL

(All:)

עַל אַרְצֵינוּ וְעַל נַחֲלַת אֲבוֹתֵינוּ
נוֹדֶה לְךָ, יְיָ, אֱלֹהֵינוּ,
שֶׁהִנְחַלְתָּנוּ וְהִנְחַלְתָּ אֶת אֲבוֹתֵינוּ
אֶרֶץ חֶמְדָּה טוֹבָה וּרְחָבָה,
בְּרִית, וְתוֹרָה, וְחַיִּים וּמָזוֹן,
וְעַל שֶׁהוֹצֵאתָנוּ מִמִּצְרַיִם,
וּפְדִיתָנוּ מִבֵּית עֲבָדִים,

וְעַל תּוֹרָתְךָ שֶׁלִּמַּדְתָּנוּ,
וְעַל הַכֹּל, יְיָ, אֱלֹהֵינוּ, אֲנַחְנוּ מוֹדִים לָךְ,
וּמְבָרְכִים אֶת שְׁמָךְ.
יִתְבָּרַךְ שִׁמְךָ תָּמִיד לְעוֹלָם וָעֶד, כָּאָמוּר:
"וְאָכַלְתָּ וְשָׂבָעְתָּ וּבֵרַכְתָּ אֶת יְיָ אֱלֹהֶיךָ."
בָּרוּךְ אַתָּה, יְיָ עַל הָאָרֶץ וְעַל הַמָּזוֹן.

For our land, and our ancestral inheritance,
We thank You, Adonai, our God,
For bequeathing to us and to our ancestors
   A delightful, good and bountiful land,
   A covenant, Torah, life and food;
And for delivering us from Egypt
   and redeeming us from bondage;
And for the Torah that you taught us;
For everything, Adonai, our God,
   we thank You,
   and bless your name.
Let your name be blessed forever and ever,
As it is written (Deuteronomy 8:10):
   "When you eat and are satisfied,
   bless Adonai your God."
Blessed are You, Adonai, for the land and
   for its food.

BLESSING OF JERUSALEM

(All:)

נַחֲמֵינוּ, יְיָ, אֱלֹהֵינוּ, בְּצִיּוֹן עִירֶךָ בְּרִנָּה,
וְרַחֵם, יְיָ, אֱלֹהֵינוּ,
עָלֵינוּ,
וְעַל יִשְׂרָאֵל עַמֶּךָ,
וְעַל יְרוּשָׁלַיִם עִירֶךָ,
וְעַל צִיּוֹן מִשְׁכַּן כְּבוֹדֶךָ,
וְעַל מַלְכוּת בֵּית דָּוִד מְשִׁיחֶךָ.
בִּמְהֵרָה תַּחֲזִירֶנָּה לִמְקוֹמָהּ, כִּי לְךָ, יְיָ,
מְיַחֲלוֹת עֵינֵינוּ.
וְתִבְנֶה צִיּוֹן עִיר קָדְשֶׁךָ, וְתִמְלוֹךְ עָלֵינוּ אַתָּה לְבַדֶּךָ,
וְתוֹשִׁיעֵנוּ לְמַעַן שְׁמֶךָ.
וְאַף עַל פִּי שֶׁאָכַלְנוּ וְשָׁתִינוּ,

חֻרְבַּן בֵּיתְךָ הַגָּדוֹל וְהַקָּדוֹשׁ לֹא שְׁכַחֲנוּ.
וְאַל תִּשְׁכָּחֵנוּ לָעַד
כִּי חָסִיד וְקָדוֹשׁ וּבָרוּךְ וְנֶאֱמָן אַתָּה, וְנֶאֱמַר:
"בּוֹנֵה יְרוּשָׁלַיִם יְיָ נִדְחֵי יִשְׂרָאֵל יְכַנֵּס."
בָּרוּךְ אַתָּה, יְיָ, הַבּוֹנֶה בְרַחֲמָיו אֶת יְרוּשָׁלַיִם.

Comfort us, Adonai, our God, in Zion, your city,
    With joy.
Have mercy, Adonai, our God,
    On us
    On Israel, your people,
    On Jerusalem, your city,
    On Zion, the dwelling place of your glory,
    And on the dominion of the house of David
        your messiah.
Quickly restore it to its place,
For we look only to You.
We have just eaten and drunk our fill,
But we have not forgotten the destruction
    of your great and holy house.
Do not ever forget it, yourself,
For You are pious, holy, blessed and faithful,
As it is written (Psalm 147:2),
"Adonai will build Jerusalem and restore
    the exiles of Israel."
Blessed are You, Adonai, for building Jerusalem
    in mercy.

BLESSING OF GOOD TIDINGS

(All:)

בָּרוּךְ אַתָּה, יְיָ, אֱלֹהֵינוּ מֶלֶךְ הָעוֹלָם,
תִּתְבָּרַךְ לָעַד
הָאֵל אָבִינוּ, מַלְכֵּנוּ, מַחֲסֵינוּ, תּוֹחַלְתֵּינוּ,
קְדוֹשֵׁינוּ, קְדוֹשׁ יַעֲקֹב.
רוֹעֵנוּ, וְרוֹעֵה יִשְׂרָאֵל,
הַמֶּלֶךְ הָרַחֲמָן, הַטּוֹב וְהַמֵּטִיב,
הָאֵל אֲשֶׁר בְּכָל יוֹם וָיוֹם
הוּא מַרְבֶּה לְהֵיטִיב לָנוּ.
הוּא גְמָלָנוּ,

הוּא גוֹמְלֵנוּ,
הוּא עָתִיד יִגְמְלֵנוּ לָעַד
חֵן וָחֶסֶד וְהַצְלָחָה וְכָל טוֹב.
הָרַחֲמָן יִמְלוֹךְ לְעוֹלָם וָעֶד.
הָרַחֲמָן יִתְעַלֶּה לְדוֹרֵי דוֹרִים.
הָרַחֲמָן קֶרֶן לְעַמּוֹ יָרִים.
הָרַחֲמָן יְחַיֵּינוּ וִיזַכֵּנוּ לִימוֹת הַמָּשִׁיחַ
וּלְחַיֵּי הָעוֹלָם הַבָּא.

Blessed are you, Adonai, our God, ruler of the
   universe.
Be blessed forever,
   Our God, parent and ruler,
   Our protector and hope
   Our holy One, the holy One of Jacob.
   Our shepherd, the shepherd of Israel
   Our merciful monarch,
      who is good and does good
   Our God who daily multiplies our good fortune.
You have rewarded us in the past,
You reward us even now,
You will reward us in the future,
   with grace, compassion, success and
   all good things.

May the all-merciful One reign forever.
May the all-merciful One be exalted for
   all generations.
May the all-merciful One raise a horn of plenty
   for our people.
May the all-merciful One grant us life, and
   let us merit a messianic time and life in the
   world to come.
Amen.

(It is customary here to pause long enough to allow anyone who wishes to offer extemporaneous prayers, beginning
with, "May the all-merciful . . ." after which all assembled
answer, "Amen.")

May the all-merciful. . . . Amen.

CONCLUSION

עֹשֶׂה שָׁלוֹם בִּמְרוֹמָיו, הוּא יַעֲשֶׂה שָׁלוֹם עָלֵינוּ
וְעַל כָּל יִשְׂרָאֵל, וְאִמְרוּ אָמֵן.

Oseh shalom bimromav
Hu ya'aseh shalom aleinu
V'al kol yisra'el
V'imru amen.

May the One who makes peace on high,
grant peace also to us, and to all Israel.
To which we say,
Amen.

Notes

SECTION THREE
How to Shape Sacred Time

1. Sometimes the book has endnotes, like this one. They are included to give you the chance to think through some of the spiritual insight behind the blessing. Do not stop to read endnotes while you are saying the blessing. But some time later, in your hotel room that night, perhaps, read the endnote with the blessing again. This will help you recollect the experience while it is still fresh in your memory. You will be able to reflect on a deeper understanding of what the blessing and the event may mean.

2. From the daily morning service; originally for a blessing for awakening to the dawn of a new day.

3. A reversal of the daily morning blessing *zokef kefufim,* "who raises up the fallen."

4. From the blessing that is traditionally said upon completing a journey safely.

5. From Jeremiah 33:10–11, a messianic promise of days to come.

6. From an ancient prayer used in the land of Israel; an old version of the *Amidah.*

7. From the service surrounding the Torah, but based on *Lamentations.*

SECTION FOUR
This Place Is Holy

1. The various *aliyot* (waves of immigration) are divided as follows: First Aliyah (1882–1903), some 25,000 individuals and small groups, many of whom returned home in bitter failure. Second

Aliyah (1904–1914), largely from Russia, prompted to some extent by the Kishinev pogroms of 1903 and 1905, when the Czarist government supported wide-scale Jewish massacres, demonstrating to the Zionists that Jews should build up a Jewish homeland, above all else. Third Aliyah (1919–1923), again from eastern Europe, occasioned by the widespread destruction to Jewish communities devastated by World War I. Fourth Aliyah (1924–1928), mostly from Poland, and more urban than prior *aliyot,* a response to anti-Semitic outbreaks occasioned by the rise of post-war Polish nationalism. Fifth Aliyah (1929–1939), Jews fleeing the rise of Nazism. Some historians describe a Sixth and Seventh Aliyah also, referring those Jews who arrived during and after World War II. Certainly the recent arrival of Jews from Russia and Ethiopia are independent *aliyot* in their own right.

2. Frances Burnce, ed., *A. D. Gordon: Selected Essays* (Boston: Independent Press, 1938) and Simon Noveck, ed., *Contemporary Jewish Thought: A Reader* (Clinton, Mass.: Colonial Press, 1963).

3. Based on Jeremiah 31:19, "Ephraim is a dear son to me." The poet inserts Abraham for Ephraim and plays on his name, as well as that of the patriarch, Abraham, who follows God's command to "Go to the Land that I will show you." The passage in Jeremiah describes Ephraim (Joseph's son, and another name for Israel generally) as beloved to God; surely Abraham is also.

4. Based on Psalm 90:17, "Establish the work of our hands."

5. Ben-Zvi, Rachel Yanait, *Before Golda: Manya Shochat: A Biography,* Trans. Sandra Shurin. (New York: Biblio Press, 1989.)

6. Isaac Luria introduced liturgical meditations called *kavvanot,* in which he focused on the mystical intention behind the prayers. Our common notion of *tikkun olam* ("repairing the world"), though known to the Rabbis of antiquity, reemerged with Luria with the specific meaning of transforming the experience of fragmentation into perfect wholeness. In one way or another, that thought precedes all kabbalistic prayer and is also the ground for Chasidic spirituality.

7. From Lawrence Fine, *Safed Spirituality* (New York: Paulist Press, 1984).

8. The blessing appears first in the ancient Temple cult, from which it was taken over in the standard liturgy, where it appears several times. The introduction to the blessing is known as a *kavvanah.* Originally *kavvanah* meant "intention," paying attention to what was being said in prayer and not reciting words by rote. Kabbalistic thought converted the word into a technical term: the name for a meditation that precedes a mitzvah and draws our attention to its deeper mystical meaning. Believing

that God is somehow both male and female, they applied the term *Sh'khinah*, originally just a word for God's presence, to the feminine side of God. They believed that their performance of mitzvot served to reunite a divided deity into perfect harmony. Since the advanced notion of *kavvanah* had its origin at Safed, where above all, redemption was the focus of all prayers, the visit to Safed is accompanied by a prayer for redemption and the preceding *kavvanah*.

9. From the liturgy of Yom Kippur.

10. This translation of the Song of Songs is my own, but I have benefitted from Marcia Falk, *The Song of Songs: A New Translation (Love Lyrics from the Bible)* (New York: HarperSanFrancisco, 1993).

11. The traditional blessing from the daily *Amidah*, praying for agricultural abundance.

12. A play on words from Isaiah 40:3, which read, "A voice cries out, 'In the desert, clear a road . . .'" But it can be read, "A voice cries out in the desert: 'Clear a road . . .'" This blessing, new here, captures the sense of the work of restoring the desert to life as heeding a command heard here in the desert itself. It recollects also God's paradigmatic appearance to Moses at the burning bush and, at Sinai, to all of Israel—both of them desert experiences.

13. Israel T. Na'amani, David Rudavky, and Abraham I. Katch, eds., *Israel Through the Eyes of Its Leaders* (Tel Aviv: Meorot, 1971). I am also indebted to Michael Keren, *Ben-Gurion and the Intellectuals* (DeKalb, IL: Northern Illinois Press, 1983).

14. From an ancient prayer used in the land of Israel; an old version of the *Amidah*; applied here with reference to David Ben-Gurion.

15. The last two lines of the familiar liturgical poem *Adon Olam*, intended as a statement of faith in God even when we sleep our final sleep of death; followed by a traditional blessing affirming God's care for our people at all times.

16. Ronald Sanders, *The High Walls of Jerusalem* (New York: Holt, Rinehart and Winston, Inc., 1983).

17. A combination of the saying attributed to Rabbi Nachman of Bratslav and Psalm 118:5, both of which deal with strait places; followed by Psalm 126, which was recited by Chief Rabbi Hertz at the celebration by British Jews, following the announcement of the Balfour Declaration.

18. Adapted from the daily liturgy: the seventeenth benediction of the *Amidah*.

19. *Psalm 36: A Psalm Touching Genealogy.*

20. Psalm 135:21.

21. Raphael Patai, ed., Harry Zohn, trans., *The Complete Diaries of Theodor Herzl* (New York and London: Herzl Press & Thomas Yoseloff, 1960).

22. The traditional prayer recited upon visiting a grave.

23. Translation based on that which is provided by Cecil Roth, ed., *Encyclopedia Judaica*.

24. Illegal immigrants, generally smuggled past British border patrols.

25. Taken from the conclusion of the *Kaddish*.

26. Abraham Joshua Heschel, *Israel: An Echo of Eternity* (Woodstock, Vt.: Jewish Lights Publishing, 1997).

27. A prayer drawn from Abraham Joshua Heschel, and *Sha'arei Dim'ah*, a collection of traditional prayers for recitation at the Wall.

28. Based on the blessing for the pilgrimage festivals. The reference "rise up" points to the smoke of the sacrificial offering that prompted the prayer in the first place.

29. An ancient blessing attibuted by the Rabbis to the Temple's sacrificial cult. It was used regularly by Jews in Israel until the Crusades, and adopted anew by Reform Judaism's *Union Prayer Book*.

30. Gershom Scholem, *From Berlin to Jerusalem: Memories of My Youth* (New York: Schocken, 1980).

31. The traditional blessing to be said in the presence of a secular scholar.

32. From the standard morning prayers, recited when arising.

33. From the *Bet Ha-Shitah Kibbutz Haggadah,* 1947. The poem appears in Hebrew in Yosef Hayim Yerushalmi, *Haggadah and History* (Philadelphia: Jewish Publication Society, 1975). Translation here provided by Joel M. Hoffman.

34. *Yizkor* and *El Malei Rachamim*, the two prayers associated with memorializing the dead, and customary at all memorial services. The first was composed after the slaughter of Rhineland Jewry by the Crusaders in 1096; the second was written as a response to pogroms in the Ukraine in 1648. English versions are taken from *Gates of Repentance*, the High Holy Days prayer book of the Reform Movement.

35. From the daily morning liturgy.

36. From ancient fast day liturgy, when the Temple still stood.

37. Information drawn from Manfred Waserman and Amalie Moses Kass, "Moses Montefiore, a Hebrew Prayer Book, and Medicine in the Holy Land," *Judaism* 45 (1996): 324–32.

38. Borrowed from an insertion in the daily *Amidah*.

39. Psalm verses traditionally said to commemorate the death of Moses. These are normally said during to the Shabbat afternoon *(minchah)* synagogue service, because of the tradition that Moses died then. This translation is borrowed largely from *Siddur Sim Shalom*.

40. The traditional blessing for hearing news of a death, and for performing *k'riyah,* the ritual of cutting the ribbon or one's clothes at the funeral of immediate family members. Used also, by some, when lighting a *Yizkor* (memorial) lamp.

41. A combination of the traditional prayer customarily said in synagogue during the reading of the Torah, and the blessing assigned to the liturgy for the Sabbath that precedes each new month. Translations are based on those of *Siddur Sim Shalom*, the prayer book of the Conservative Movement.

42. The traditional blessing for seeing the Mediterranean.

43. From an ancient prayer from *Eretz Yisrael*, adopted by Italian Jewry, and then lost; recovered here for use in pilgrimages to the land where it was created.

44. From the *haftarah* blessings for Shabbat and an ancient blessing recited on fast days when the Temple still stood.

45. From a prayer first recorded in the ninth century, and customarily said to this day when people are called to the Torah.

46. From an ancient prayer on fast days, when the Temple still stood.

47. From the daily liturgy, the ninth benediction of the *Amidah*.

S E C T I O N   F I V E

The Guide to Blessing

1. From the blessing preceding the morning recitation of the *Sh'ma* in the daily liturgy.

2. A combination of the traditional prayer for blessing, customarily said in a synagogue during the reading of the Torah, and the prayer for blessing assigned to the liturgy for the Shabbat that precedes each new month. Translations are based on those of *Siddur Sim*

Shalom, the prayer book of the Conservative movement.

3. From Talmud *Berakhot* 54a.

4. From the Siddur, a prayer associated with the act of Torah study.

5. Numbers 23:8; 20; 24:5.

6. The words for "sacred center" are biblical; they refer to the center of the ancient temple, the place that our ancestors believed was literally the axis of the world.

7. Format of the *Kaddish* with places interspersed is borrowed from *Siddur Sim Shalom,* the prayer book of the Conservative movement.

8. Translation is based on the version supplied in *Gates of Prayer,* the prayer book for the Reform movement.

9. The traditional blessing prescribed for standing in the presence of a Torah scholar; adapted here for recitation in places of wisdom.

10. The words of *Hatikvah* were written in 1878 by the poet Naftali Hertz Imber to celebrate the founding of the first Jewish settlement in Palestine, Petach Tikvah. In 1882, malaria had all but killed the first wave of settlers there, but Imber came to Israel and read the poem to farmers in nearby Rishon L'tsiyon. That very year, or shortly thereafter, Samuel Cohen, a recent immigrant who heard the poem, set it to music based on a Romanian folk melody. It was sung here and there, but became well known in 1905 when the Seventh Zionist Congress meeting in Basel ended with the song. In 1933 it was declared the Zionist national anthem.

At first, the last four lines read: "Our hope is not yet lost / The age-old hope / To return to the land of our fathers / To the city where David dwelt." With the founding of the state in 1948, the lyrics were changed to reflect the fact that the return had actually begun.

11. Blessing based on Jeremiah 17:13, "God is the hope of Israel."

12. A new blessing but based on the instructions in the Talmud to follow the interests of peace regarding relationships with non-Jews.

13. From the Midrash, *Avot d'Rabbi Natan* 2:31.

14. From the Talmud, *Ta'anit* 23a.

15. Based on a verse from the story of creation, Genesis 2:9.

16. From the Talmud, *Berakhot* 40b.

17. From the Palestinian Talmud, *Berakhot* 10:11.

18. From the Talmud, *Berakhot* 40b.

19. An ancient form of the *Birkat Hamazon* (Grace after Meals) intended especially for food that is grown in the land of Israel. We still recite it regularly at the Passover Seder. The reference to "who is good and does good" reflects the messianic hope implicit in every Jewish meal—that God may someday provide food for all. In keeping with that hope, a final line has been appended to the blessing here. The line occurs elsewhere independently as a blessing for hearing "good tidings" and therefore is messianic as well. It found its way into the traditional *Birkat Hamazon* also, so it is an appropriate conclusion.

20. English translation of *T'fillat Haderekh,* traditional prayer for a journey, from Talmud, *Berakhot* 29b. Hebrew is newly adapted by Joel M. Hoffman. For traditional Hebrew of *T'fillat Haderekh,* see p. 223.

21. *T'fillat Haderekh,* traditional prayer for a journey, from Talmud, *Berakhot* 29b.

22. Traditional prayers from the daily liturgy.

23. Prayers taken from Talmud, *Berakhot* 60b; and from traditional liturgy, the last two lines of *Adon Olam.*

24. An ancient blessing from *Eretz Yisrael* that we no longer say in our daily prayers, but is recovered here for use while visiting Israel.

S E C T I O N   S I X

A Meal in Jerusalem

1. The vitality of Jewish life in the land of Israel is particularly evident in its remarkable medieval prayer life. History proved kinder to Babylonian Jews, however; their worship service became the basis for what Jews do today, whereas Palestinian prayers were lost until the turn of the twentieth century. Only then did scholars discover a cache of manuscripts that included fragments of the prayers of Jews in *Eretz Yisrael.* This *Birkat Hamazon* is based on those manuscripts. It is a conglomerate assembled from the dazzling variety of compositions that typified Jewish life there prior to the Crusades.

  Birkat Hamazon (Grace after Meals) is among our oldest prayers. It begins with an invitation, and is followed by four separate blessings thanking God for food in general, our land of Israel, Jerusalem, and good tidings to come—the messianic age. The entire set of prayers was probably messianic in that they thank God not just for what we already have, but for what we trust God will some day provide.

Index of Places and Occasions for Which Prayers Are Provided

Absalom's tomb   162
Airplane, prayers for traveling in   221, 223
Aliyah, place of (see *Merkaz K'litah*)   199
Alkabetz, Solomon (grave of)   94
Allenby Bridge   122
Archeological remains of pagan worship, blessing at   221
Arriving in Israel   76
  Leaving home (prayer on the airplane)   221
  Upon arrival   76
Beauty, place of   200
Beit Hat'futsot (Museum of the Diaspora)   193
Bet Shean (Roman ampitheatre in),   89
Bethlehem   179
Birkat Hamazon (Grace after Meals) for *Eretz Yisrael*   230
Blessing, place of   201
Blossoming trees or shrubs, blessing for   220
Cemetery of *chalutzim* (pioneers)   84
Christian worship, place of   213
Dead Sea   100
Deganya, kibbutz in the Galil   84
Ein Gedi   104
En Dor (kibbutz)   89
First night's sleep in Israel   78
Friends or relatives, prayer for seeing   219
Galil (Galilee)   83
Grace after Meals, see *Birkat Hamazon*   230
Hadassah Hospital   157
Haifa   187
Har Herzl   136

Hebrew University   158
Hebrew, on seeing and hearing   213
Hebron   179
Herzl, Theodor (grave of)   136
Hope, place of   212
Jaffa Gate   127
Jerusalem and vicinity   121
Jerusalem, arriving in for first time   76
Jerusalem, road from airport to   76
Jewish quarter of Old City   132
Jezreel Valley   89
Kibbutz, prayers for eating at   217
Kinneret (Sea of Galilee)   84
Knesset   140
Kotel (the Wall)   146
Luria, Isaac (the Ari), grave of   94
M'apilim ship (in Haifa)   187
Maccabean homes (inside the Jaffa Gate)   132
Masada   117
   synagogue in   117
Mediterranean Sea   184
Merchavia   89
Merkaz K'litah (Absorption Center)   199
Miracle, place of   202
Mount Carmel   187
Mount Gilboa   89
Mount Nebo   174
Mount Scopus   157
Muslim worship, place of   213
Negev, the   99
   kibbutz in   109
New homes in Israel's wasteland, prayer for seeing   221
New moon, blessing for   220
Old Jerusalem   132
People who demonstrate love of the land, prayer for   220
Rabin, Yitzchak (grave of)   136
Rain, blessing for   219
Rainbow, blessing for   219
Recent tragedy, place of   207
Safed   94
Sedeh Boker (David Ben-Gurion's Home)   113

Sea of Galilee (*Kinneret*)   84

Shabbat prior to leaving   57

   at Shabbat table   57

   in synagogue   58

Sodom   100

Southern wall to the Temple Mount   153

Study, place of   203

Synagogue, new or old (praying in)   205

Tel Aviv   193

Temple Mount   149

T'fillat Haderekh, (Prayer for a safe journey)   221, 222, 223

Thunder, lightning, or a violent windstorm,

   blessing for   220

Tomb of Rachel (in Bethlehem)   180

Tombs of the patriarchs and matriarchs (in Hebron)   179

Trees, prayers for planting   214

Valley of Communities (in Yad Vashem)   167

Valley of Hinnom (Gehinom)   162

Valley of Jehoshaphat   162

Valley of Kidron   162

Valleys of Jerusalem   161

Waking up and going to bed, prayers for   224

War, place of   211

Windmill, The (of Yemin Moshe)   171

Wisdom, place of   210

Wonders of nature, blessing for   219

Yad Vashem   165

Yemin Moshe   171

Bible Study / Midrash

Passing Life's Tests
Spiritual Reflections on the Trial of Abraham, the Binding of Isaac
By Rabbi Bradley Shavit Artson, DHL
Invites us to use this powerful tale as a tool for our own soul wrestling, to confront our existential sacrifices and enable us to face—and surmount—life's tests.
6 x 9, 176 pp, Quality PB, 978-1-58023-631-7 **$18.99**

The Messiah and the Jews
Three Thousand Years of Tradition, Belief and Hope
By Rabbi Elaine Rose Glickman; Foreword by Rabbi Neil Gillman, PhD;
Preface by Rabbi Judith Z. Abrams, PhD
Explores and explains an astonishing range of primary and secondary sources, infusing them with new meaning for the modern reader.
6 x 9, 192 pp, Quality PB, 978-1-58023-690-4 **$16.99**

Speaking Torah
Spiritual Teachings from around the Maggid's Table—in Two Volumes
By Arthur Green, with Ebn Leader, Ariel Evan Mayse and Or N. Rose
The most powerful Hasidic teachings made accessible—from some of the world's preeminent authorities on Jewish thought and spirituality.
Volume 1—6 x 9, 512 pp, Hardcover, 978-1-58023-668-3 **$34.99**
Volume 2—6 x 9, 448 pp, Hardcover, 978-1-58023-694-2 **$34.99**

Masking and Unmasking Ourselves
Interpreting Biblical Texts on Clothing & Identity
By Dr. Norman J. Cohen
Presents ten Bible stories that involve clothing in an essential way, as a means of learning about the text, its characters and their interactions.
6 x 9, 224 pp, HC, 978-1-58023-461-0 **$24.99**

Hineini in Our Lives
Learning How to Respond to Others through 14 Biblical Texts and Personal Stories
By Rabbi Norman J. Cohen, PhD
6 x 9, 240 pp, Quality PB, 978-1-58023-274-6 **$18.99**

The Modern Men's Torah Commentary
New Insights from Jewish Men on the 54 Weekly Torah Portions
Edited by Rabbi Jeffrey K. Salkin
6 x 9, 368 pp, HC, 978-1-58023-395-8 **$24.99**

Moses and the Journey to Leadership
Timeless Lessons of Effective Management from the Bible and Today's Leaders
By Rabbi Norman J. Cohen, PhD
6 x 9, 240 pp, Quality PB, 978-1-58023-351-4 **$18.99**
HC, 978-1-58023-227-2 **$21.99**

The Other Talmud—The Yerushalmi
Unlocking the Secrets of The Talmud of Israel for Judaism Today
By Rabbi Judith Z. Abrams, PhD
6 x 9, 256 pp, HC, 978-1-58023-463-4 **$24.99**

Sage Tales
Wisdom and Wonder from the Rabbis of the Talmud
By Rabbi Burton L. Visotzky
6 x 9, 256 pp, Quality PB, 978-1-58023-791-8 **$19.99**; HC, 978-1-58023-456-6 **$24.99**

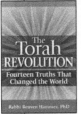

The Torah Revolution
Fourteen Truths That Changed the World
By Rabbi Reuven Hammer, PhD
6 x 9, 240 pp, HC, 978-1-58023-457-3 **$24.99**

The Wisdom of Judaism
An Introduction to the Values of the Talmud
By Rabbi Dov Peretz Elkins
6 x 9, 192 pp, Quality PB, 978-1-58023-327-9 **$16.99**

Or phone, fax, mail or email to:
JEWISH LIGHTS Publishing
An imprint of Turner Publishing Company
4507 Charlotte Avenue • Suite 100 • Nashville, TN 37209
Tel: (615) 255-2265 • www.jewishlights.com
Prices subject to change.

Spirituality / Crafts

Jewish Threads
A Hands-On Guide to Stitching Spiritual Intention into Jewish Fabric Crafts
By Diana Drew with Robert Grayson
Learn how to make your own Jewish fabric crafts with spiritual intention—a journey of creativity, imagination and inspiration. Thirty projects.
7 x 9, 288 pp, 8-page color insert, b/w illus.,
Quality PB Original, 978-1-58023-442-9 **$19.99**

Beading—The Creative Spirit
Finding Your Sacred Center through the Art of Beadwork
By Wendy Ellsworth
Invites you on a spiritual pilgrimage into the kaleidoscope world of glass and color.
7 x 9, 240 pp, 8-page full-color insert, b/w photos and diagrams
Quality PB, 978-1-59473-267-6 **$18.99***

Contemplative Crochet
A Hands-On Guide for Interlocking Faith and Craft
By Cindy Crandall-Frazier; Foreword by Linda Skolnik
Will take you on a path deeper into your crocheting and your spiritual awareness.
7 x 9, 208 pp, b/w photos, Quality PB, 978-1-59473-238-6 **$16.99***

The Knitting Way
A Guide to Spiritual Self-Discovery
By Linda Skolnik and Janice MacDaniels
Shows how to use knitting to strengthen your spiritual self.
7 x 9, 240 pp, b/w photos, Quality PB, 978-1-59473-079-5 **$16.99***

The Painting Path
Embodying Spiritual Discovery through Yoga, Brush and Color
By Linda Novick; Foreword by Richard Segalman
Explores the divine connection you can experience through art.
7 x 9, 208 pp, 8-page full-color insert, b/w photos
Quality PB, 978-1-59473-226-3 **$18.99***

The Quilting Path
A Guide to Spiritual Self-Discovery through Fabric, Thread and Kabbalah
By Louise Silk
Explores how to cultivate personal growth through quilt making.
7 x 9, 192 pp, b/w photos, Quality PB, 978-1-59473-206-5 **$16.99***

History

On the Chocolate Trail
A Delicious Adventure Connecting Jews, Religions, History, Travel, Rituals and Recipes to the Magic of Cacao
By Rabbi Deborah R. Prinz
Take a delectable journey through the religious history of chocolate—a real treat!
6 x 9, 272 pp w/ 20+ b/w photographs, Quality PB, 978-1-58023-487-0 **$18.99**

Twelve Steps

Recovery—The Sacred Art
The Twelve Steps as Spiritual Practice
By Rami Shapiro; Foreword by Joan Borysenko, PhD
Draws on insights and practices of different religious traditions to help you move more deeply into the universal spirituality of the Twelve Step system.
5½ x 8½, 240 pp, Quality PB Original, 978-1-59473-259-1 **$16.99***

Recovery from Codependence
A Jewish Twelve Steps Guide to Healing Your Soul
By Rabbi Kerry M. Olitzky
6 x 9, 160 pp, Quality PB, 978-1-879045-32-3 **$13.95**

Twelve Jewish Steps to Recovery, 2nd Edition
A Personal Guide to Turning from Alcoholism & Other Addictions—Drugs, Food, Gambling, Sex...
By Rabbi Kerry M. Olitzky and Stuart A. Copans, MD; Preface by Abraham J. Twerski, MD
6 x 9, 160 pp, Quality PB, 978-1-58023-409-2 **$16.99**

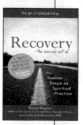

Spirituality

Amazing Chesed: Living a Grace-Filled Judaism
By Rabbi Rami Shapiro Drawing from ancient and contemporary, traditional and non-traditional Jewish wisdom, reclaims the idea of grace in Judaism.
6 x 9, 176 pp, Quality PB, 978-1-58023-624-9 **$16.99**

Jewish with Feeling: A Guide to Meaningful Jewish Practice
By Rabbi Zalman Schachter-Shalomi with Joel Segel
Takes off from basic questions like "Why be Jewish?" and whether the word God still speaks to us today and lays out a vision for a whole-person Judaism.
5½ x 8½, 288 pp, Quality PB, 978-1-58023-691-1 **$19.99**

Perennial Wisdom for the Spiritually Independent
Sacred Teachings—Annotated & Explained *Annotation by Rami Shapiro; Foreword by Richard Rohr*
Weaves sacred texts and teachings from the world's major religions into a coherent exploration of the five core questions at the heart of every religion's search.
5½ x 8½, 336 pp, Quality PB Original, 978-1-59473-515-8 **$16.99**

Mussar Yoga
Blending an Ancient Jewish Spiritual Practice with Yoga to Transform Body and Soul
By Edith R. Brotman, PhD, RYT-500; Foreword by Alan Morinis
A clear and easy-to-use introduction to an embodied spiritual practice for anyone seeking profound and lasting self-transformation.
7 x 9, 224 pp, w/ over 40 b/w photos, Quality PB, 978-1-58023-784-0 **$18.99**

Aleph-Bet Yoga: Embodying the Hebrew Letters for Physical and Spiritual Well-Being
By Steven A. Rapp; Foreword by Tamar Frankiel, PhD, and Judy Greenfeld; Preface by Hart Lazer
7 x 10, 128 pp, b/w photos, Quality PB, Lay-flat binding, 978-1-58023-162-6 **$16.95**

A Book of Life: Embracing Judaism as a Spiritual Practice
By Rabbi Michael Strassfeld 6 x 9, 544 pp, Quality PB, 978-1-58023-247-0 **$24.99**

Bringing the Psalms to Life: How to Understand and Use the Book of Psalms
By Rabbi Daniel F. Polish, PhD 6 x 9, 208 pp, Quality PB, 978-1-58023-157-2 **$18.99**

Does the Soul Survive? A Jewish Journey to Belief in Afterlife, Past Lives & Living with Purpose
By Rabbi Elie Kaplan Spitz; Foreword by Brian L. Weiss, MD
6 x 9, 288 pp, Quality PB, 978-1-58023-165-7 **$18.99**

Entering the Temple of Dreams: Jewish Prayers, Movements and Meditations for the End of the Day
By Tamar Frankiel, PhD, and Judy Greenfeld
7 x 10, 192 pp, illus., Quality PB, 978-1-58023-079-7 **$16.95**

First Steps to a New Jewish Spirit: Reb Zalman's Guide to Recapturing the Intimacy & Ecstasy in Your Relationship with God
By Rabbi Zalman M. Schachter-Shalomi with Donald Gropman
6 x 9, 144 pp, Quality PB, 978-1-58023-182-4 **$16.95**

Foundations of Sephardic Spirituality: The Inner Life of Jews of the Ottoman Empire
By Rabbi Marc D. Angel, PhD
6 x 9, 224 pp, Quality PB, 978-1-58023-341-5 **$18.99**

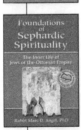

God & the Big Bang: Discovering Harmony between Science & Spirituality
By Dr. Daniel C. Matt 6 x 9, 216 pp, Quality PB, 978-1-879045-89-7 **$18.99**

God in Our Relationships: Spirituality between People from the Teachings of Martin Buber
By Rabbi Dennis S. Ross 5½ x 8½, 160 pp, Quality PB, 978-1-58023-147-3 **$16.95**

The Jewish Lights Spirituality Handbook: A Guide to Understanding, Exploring & Living a Spiritual Life
Edited by Stuart M. Matlins 6 x 9, 456 pp, Quality PB, 978-1-58023-093-3 **$19.99**

Judaism, Physics and God
Searching for Sacred Metaphors in a Post-Einstein World
By Rabbi David W. Nelson
6 x 9, 352 pp, Quality PB, inc. reader's discussion guide,
978-1-58023-306-4 **$18.99**; HC, 352 pp, 978-1-58023-252-4 **$24.99**

Tanya, the Masterpiece of Hasidic Wisdom
Selections Annotated & Explained
Translation & Annotation by Rabbi Rami Shapiro; Foreword by Rabbi Zalman M. Schachter-Shalomi
5½ x 8½, 240 pp, Quality PB, 978-1-59473-275-1 **$16.99**

These Are the Words, 2nd Edition
A Vocabulary of Jewish Spiritual Life
By Rabbi Arthur Green, PhD
6 x 9, 320 pp, Quality PB, 978-1-58023-494-8 **$19.99**

Theology / Philosophy / The Way Into... Series

The Way Into Encountering God in Judaism
By Rabbi Neil Gillman, PhD
For everyone who wants to understand how Jews have encountered God throughout history and today.
6 x 9, 240 pp, Quality PB, 978-1-58023-199-2 **$18.99**
HC, 978-1-58023-025-4 **$21.95**
Also Available: **The Jewish Approach to God:** A Brief Introduction for Christians
By Rabbi Neil Gillman, PhD
5½ x 8½, 192 pp, Quality PB, 978-1-58023-190-9 **$16.95**

The Way Into Jewish Mystical Tradition
By Rabbi Lawrence Kushner
Allows readers to interact directly with the sacred mystical texts of the Jewish tradition. An accessible introduction to the concepts of Jewish mysticism, their religious and spiritual significance, and how they relate to life today.
6 x 9, 224 pp, Quality PB, 978-1-58023-200-5 **$18.99**

The Way Into Jewish Prayer
By Rabbi Lawrence A. Hoffman, PhD
Opens the door to 3,000 years of Jewish prayer, making anyone feel at home in the Jewish way of communicating with God.
6 x 9, 208 pp, Quality PB, 978-1-58023-201-2 **$18.99**
The Way Into Jewish Prayer Teacher's Guide
By Rabbi Jennifer Ossakow Goldsmith
8½ x 11, 42 pp, PB, 978-1-58023-345-3 **$8.99**
Download a free copy at www.jewishlights.com.

The Way Into Judaism and the Environment
By Jeremy Benstein, PhD
Explores the ways in which Judaism contributes to contemporary social-environmental issues, the extent to which Judaism is part of the problem and how it can be part of the solution.
6 x 9, 288 pp, Quality PB, 978-1-58023-368-2 **$18.99**
HC, 978-1-58023-268-5 **$24.99**

The Way Into *Tikkun Olam* (Repairing the World)
By Rabbi Elliot N. Dorff, PhD
An accessible introduction to the Jewish concept of the individual's responsibility to care for others and repair the world.
6 x 9, 304 pp, Quality PB, 978-1-58023-328-6 **$18.99**

The Way Into Torah
By Rabbi Norman J. Cohen, PhD
Helps guide you in the exploration of the origins and development of Torah, explains why it should be studied and how to do it.
6 x 9, 176 pp, Quality PB, 978-1-58023-198-5 **$16.99**

The Way Into the Varieties of Jewishness
By Sylvia Barack Fishman, PhD
Explores the religious and historical understanding of what it has meant to be Jewish from ancient times to the present controversy over "Who is a Jew?"
6 x 9, 288 pp, Quality PB, 978-1-58023-367-5 **$18.99**
HC, 978-1-58023-030-8 **$24.99**

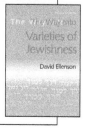

Inspiration

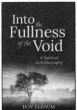

Into the Fullness of the Void: A Spiritual Autobiography
By Dov Elbaum
The spiritual autobiography of one of Israel's leading cultural figures that provides insights and guidance for all of us.
6 x 9, 304 pp, Quality PB Original, 978-1-58023-715-4 **$18.99**

Saying No and Letting Go: Jewish Wisdom on Making Room for What Matters Most
By Rabbi Edwin Goldberg, DHL; Foreword by Rabbi Naomi Levy
Timeless Jewish wisdom on how to "hold on tightly" to the things that matter most.
6 x 9, 192 pp, Quality PB, 978-1-58023-670-6 **$16.99**

The Empty Chair: Finding Hope and Joy—Timeless Wisdom from a Hasidic Master, Rebbe Nachman of Breslov
Adapted by Moshe Mykoff and the Breslov Research Institute
4 x 6, 128 pp, Deluxe PB w/ flaps, 978-1-879045-67-5 **$9.99**

The Gentle Weapon: Prayers for Everyday and Not-So-Everyday Moments—Timeless Wisdom from the Teachings of the Hasidic Master, Rebbe Nachman of Breslov
Adapted by Moshe Mykoff and S. C. Mizrahi, together with the Breslov Research Institute
4 x 6, 144 pp, Deluxe PB w/ flaps, 978-1-58023-022-3 **$9.99**

The God Upgrade: Finding Your 21st-Century Spirituality in Judaism's 5,000-Year-Old Tradition
By Rabbi Jamie Korngold; Foreword by Rabbi Harold M. Schulweis
6 x 9, 176 pp, Quality PB, 978-1-58023-443-6 **$15.99**

God Whispers: Stories of the Soul, Lessons of the Heart
By Rabbi Karyn D. Kedar
6 x 9, 176 pp, Quality PB, 978-1-58023-088-9 **$16.99**

God's To-Do List: 103 Ways to Be an Angel and Do God's Work on Earth
By Dr. Ron Wolfson 6 x 9, 144 pp, Quality PB, 978-1-58023-301-9 **$16.99**

Happiness and the Human Spirit: The Spirituality of Becoming the Best You Can Be
By Rabbi Abraham J. Twerski, MD
6 x 9, 176 pp, Quality PB, 978-1-58023-404-7 **$16.99**; HC, 978-1-58023-343-9 **$19.99**

Life's Daily Blessings: Inspiring Reflections on Gratitude and Joy for Every Day, Based on Jewish Wisdom *By Rabbi Kerry M. Olitzky*
4½ x 6½, 368 pp, Quality PB, 978-1-58023-396-5 **$16.99**

The Magic of Hebrew Chant: Healing the Spirit, Transforming the Mind, Deepening Love   *By Rabbi Shefa Gold; Foreword by Sylvia Boorstein*
6 x 9, 352 pp, Quality PB, 978-1-58023-671-3 **$24.99**

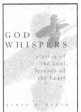

Restful Reflections: Nighttime Inspiration to Calm the Soul, Based on Jewish Wisdom
By Rabbi Kerry M. Olitzky and Rabbi Lori Forman-Jacobi
4½ x 6½, 448 pp, Quality PB, 978-1-58023-091-9 **$16.99**

Sacred Intentions: Morning Inspiration to Strengthen the Spirit, Based on Jewish Wisdom
By Rabbi Kerry M. Olitzky and Rabbi Lori Forman-Jacobi
4½ x 6½, 448 pp, Quality PB, 978-1-58023-061-2 **$16.99**

The Seven Questions You're Asked in Heaven: Reviewing and Renewing Your Life on Earth
By Dr. Ron Wolfson   6 x 9, 176 pp, Quality PB, 978-1-58023-407-8 **$16.99**

Kabbalah / Mysticism

Ehyeh: A Kabbalah for Tomorrow
By Rabbi Arthur Green, PhD 6 x 9, 224 pp, Quality PB, 978-1-58023-213-5 **$18.99**

The Gift of Kabbalah: Discovering the Secrets of Heaven, Renewing Your Life on Earth *By Tamar Frankiel, PhD* 6 x 9, 256 pp, Quality PB, 978-1-58023-141-1 **$16.95**

Jewish Mysticism and the Spiritual Life: Classical Texts, Contemporary Reflections
Edited by Dr. Lawrence Fine, Dr. Eitan Fishbane and Rabbi Or N. Rose
6 x 9, 256 pp, HC, 978-1-58023-434-4 **$24.99**; Quality PB, 978-1-58023-719-2 **$18.99**

Seek My Face: A Jewish Mystical Theology
By Rabbi Arthur Green, PhD 6 x 9, 304 pp, Quality PB, 978-1-58023-130-5 **$19.95**

Zohar: Annotated & Explained
Translation & Annotation by Dr. Daniel C. Matt; Foreword by Andrew Harvey
5½ x 8½, 176 pp, Quality PB, 978-1-893361-51-5 **$16.99**
(A book from SkyLight Paths, Jewish Lights' sister imprint)

See also *The Way Into Jewish Mystical Tradition* in The Way Into... Series.

Holidays / Holy Days

Prayers of Awe Series

An exciting new series that examines the High Holy Day liturgy to enrich the praying experience of everyone—whether experienced worshipers or guests who encounter Jewish prayer for the very first time.

All the World
Universalism, Particularism, and the High Holy Days
Edited by Rabbi Lawrence A. Hoffman, PhD
Combines the particularistic concern for Israel as a People called by God with the universalistic proclamation that Israel is called for universal ends.
6 x 9, 288 pp, HC, 978-1-58023-783-3 **$24.99**

May God Remember
Memory and Memorializing in Judaism—*Yizkor*
Edited by Rabbi Lawrence A. Hoffman, PhD
Examines the history and ideas behind *Yizkor*, the Jewish memorial service, and this fascinating chapter in Jewish piety.
6 x 9, 304 pp, HC, 978-1-58023-689-8 **$24.99**

We Have Sinned—Sin and Confession in Judaism
Ashamnu and Al Chet
Edited by Rabbi Lawrence A. Hoffman, PhD
6 x 9, 304 pp, HC, 978-1-58023-612-6 **$24.99**

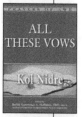

Who by Fire, Who by Water—*Un'taneh Tokef*
Edited by Rabbi Lawrence A. Hoffman, PhD
6 x 9, 272 pp, Quality PB, 978-1-58023-672-0 **$19.99**
HC, 978-1-58023-424-5 **$24.99**

All These Vows—*Kol Nidre*
Edited by Rabbi Lawrence A. Hoffman, PhD
6 x 9, 288 pp, HC, 978-1-58023-430-6 **$24.99**

Rosh Hashanah Readings
Inspiration, Information and Contemplation
Yom Kippur Readings
Inspiration, Information and Contemplation
Edited by Rabbi Dov Peretz Elkins; Section Introductions from Arthur Green's These Are the Words
Rosh Hashanah: 6 x 9, 400 pp, Quality PB, 978-1-58023-437-5 **$19.99**
Yom Kippur: 6 x 9, 368 pp, Quality PB, 978-1-58023-438-2 **$19.99**
HC, 978-1-58023-271-5 **$24.99**

Shabbat, 2nd Edition
The Family Guide to Preparing for and Celebrating the Sabbath
By Dr. Ron Wolfson
7 x 9, 320 pp, Illus., Quality PB, 978-1-58023-164-0 **$21.99**

Hanukkah, 2nd Edition
The Family Guide to Spiritual Celebration
By Dr. Ron Wolfson
7 x 9, 240 pp, Illus., Quality PB, 978-1-58023-122-0 **$18.95**

Passover

My People's Passover Haggadah
Traditional Texts, Modern Commentaries
Edited by Rabbi Lawrence A. Hoffman, PhD, and David Arnow, PhD
A diverse and exciting collection of commentaries on the traditional Passover Haggadah—in two volumes!
Vol. 1: 7 x 10, 304 pp, HC, 978-1-58023-354-5 **$24.99**
Vol. 2: 7 x 10, 320 pp, HC, 978-1-58023-346-0 **$24.99**

Creating Lively Passover Seders, 2nd Edition
A Sourcebook of Engaging Tales, Texts & Activities
By David Arnow, PhD
7 x 9, 464 pp, Quality PB, 978-1-58023-444-3 **$24.99**

Freedom Journeys
The Tale of Exodus and Wilderness across Millennia
By Rabbi Arthur O. Waskow and Rabbi Phyllis O. Berman
6 x 9, 288 pp, HC, 978-1-58023-445-0 **$24.99**

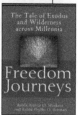

Leading the Passover Journey
The Seder's Meaning Revealed, the Haggadah's Story Retold
By Rabbi Nathan Laufer
6 x 9, 224 pp, Quality PB, 978-1-58023-399-6 **$18.99**

Passover, 2nd Edition
The Family Guide to Spiritual Celebration
By Dr. Ron Wolfson with Joel Lurie Grishaver 7 x 9, 416 pp,
Quality PB, 978-1-58023-174-9 **$19.95**

Life Cycle
Marriage / Parenting / Family / Aging

The New Jewish Baby Album: Creating and Celebrating the Beginning of a Spiritual Life—A Jewish Lights Companion
By the Editors at Jewish Lights; Foreword by Anita Diamant;
Preface by Rabbi Sandy Eisenberg Sasso
A spiritual keepsake that will be treasured for generations. More than just a memory book, *shows you how—and why it's important*—to create a Jewish home and a Jewish life.
8 x 10, 64 pp, Deluxe Padded HC, Full-color illus., 978-1-58023-138-1 **$19.95**

The Jewish Pregnancy Book: A Resource for the Soul, Body & Mind during Pregnancy, Birth & the First Three Months
By Sandy Falk, MD, and Rabbi Daniel Judson, with Steven A. Rapp
Medical information, prayers and rituals for each stage of pregnancy.
7 x 10, 208 pp, b/w photos, Quality PB, 978-1-58023-178-7 **$16.95**

Celebrating Your New Jewish Daughter: Creating Jewish Ways to Welcome Baby Girls into the Covenant—New and Traditional Ceremonies
By Debra Nussbaum Cohen; Foreword by Rabbi Sandy Eisenberg Sasso
6 x 9, 272 pp, Quality PB, 978-1-58023-090-2 **$18.95**

The New Jewish Baby Book, 2nd Edition: Names, Ceremonies & Customs—A Guide for Today's Families
By Anita Diamant
6 x 9, 320 pp, Quality PB, 978-1-58023-251-7 **$19.99**

Parenting as a Spiritual Journey: Deepening Ordinary and Extraordinary Events into Sacred Occasions
By Rabbi Nancy Fuchs-Kreimer, PhD
6 x 9, 224 pp, Quality PB, 978-1-58023-016-2 **$17.99**

Parenting Jewish Teens: A Guide for the Perplexed
By Joanne Doades Explores the questions and issues that shape the world in which today's Jewish teenagers live and offers constructive advice to parents.
6 x 9, 176 pp, Quality PB, 978-1-58023-305-7 **$16.99**

The Creative Jewish Wedding Book, 2nd Edition: A Hands-On Guide to New & Old Traditions, Ceremonies & Celebrations
By Gabrielle Kaplan-Mayer
9 x 9, 288 pp, b/w photos, Quality PB, 978-1-58023-398-9 **$19.99**

Divorce Is a Mitzvah: A Practical Guide to Finding Wholeness and Holiness When Your Marriage Dies
By Rabbi Perry Netter; Afterword by Rabbi Laura Geller
6 x 9, 224 pp, Quality PB, 978-1-58023-172-5 **$16.95**

Embracing the Covenant: Converts to Judaism Talk About Why & How
By Rabbi Allan Berkowitz and Patti Moskovitz
6 x 9, 192 pp, Quality PB, 978-1-879045-50-7 **$16.95**

A Heart of Wisdom: Making the Jewish Journey from Midlife through the Elder Years
Edited by Susan Berrin; Foreword by Rabbi Harold Kushner
6 x 9, 384 pp, Quality PB, 978-1-58023-051-3 **$18.95**

Introducing My Faith and My Community: The Jewish Outreach Institute Guide for the Christian in a Jewish Interfaith Relationship
By Rabbi Kerry M. Olitzky
6 x 9, 176 pp, Quality PB, 978-1-58023-192-3 **$16.99**

Making a Successful Jewish Interfaith Marriage: The Jewish Outreach Institute Guide to Opportunities, Challenges and Resources
By Rabbi Kerry M. Olitzky with Joan Peterson Littman
6 x 9, 176 pp, Quality PB, 978-1-58023-170-1 **$16.95**

A Man's Responsibility: A Jewish Guide to Being a Son, a Partner in Marriage, a Father and a Community Leader *By Rabbi Joseph B. Meszler*
6 x 9, 192 pp, Quality PB, 978-1-58023-435-1 **$16.99**

So That Your Values Live On: Ethical Wills and How to Prepare Them
Edited by Rabbi Jack Riemer and Rabbi Nathaniel Stampfer
6 x 9, 272 pp, Quality PB, 978-1-879045-34-7 **$18.99**

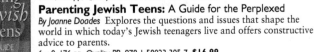

Social Justice

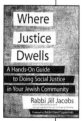

Where Justice Dwells
A Hands-On Guide to Doing Social Justice in Your Jewish Community
By Rabbi Jill Jacobs; Foreword by Rabbi David Saperstein
Provides ways to envision and act on your own ideals of social justice.
7 x 9, 288 pp, Quality PB Original, 978-1-58023-453-5 **$24.99**

There Shall Be No Needy
Pursuing Social Justice through Jewish Law and Tradition
By Rabbi Jill Jacobs; Foreword by Rabbi Elliot N. Dorff, PhD; Preface by Simon Greer
Confronts the most pressing issues of twenty-first-century America from a deeply Jewish perspective.
6 x 9, 288 pp, Quality PB, 978-1-58023-425-2 **$16.99**

There Shall Be No Needy Teacher's Guide
8½ x 11, 56 pp, PB, 978-1-58023-429-0 **$8.99**

Conscience
The Duty to Obey and the Duty to Disobey
By Rabbi Harold M. Schulweis
Examines the idea of conscience and the role conscience plays in our relationships to government, law, ethics, religion, human nature, God—and to each other.
6 x 9, 160 pp, Quality PB, 978-1-58023-419-1 **$16.99**
HC, 978-1-58023-375-0 **$19.99**

Judaism and Justice
The Jewish Passion to Repair the World
By Rabbi Sidney Schwarz; Foreword by Ruth Messinger
Explores the relationship between Judaism, social justice and the Jewish identity of American Jews.
6 x 9, 352 pp, Quality PB, 978-1-58023-353-8 **$19.99**

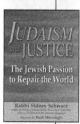

Spirituality / Women's Interest

Embracing the Divine Feminine
Finding God through the Ecstasy of Physical Love—The Song of Songs Annotated & Explained
Translation & Annotation by Rabbi Rami Shapiro
Foreword by Rev. Cynthia Bourgeault, PhD
5½ x 8½, 200 pp (est), Quality PB, 978-1-59473-575-2 **$16.99***

New Jewish Feminism
Probing the Past, Forging the Future
Edited by Rabbi Elyse Goldstein; Foreword by Anita Diamant
6 x 9, 480 pp, HC, 978-1-58023-359-0 **$24.99**

The Divine Feminine in Biblical Wisdom Literature
Selections Annotated & Explained
Translation & Annotation by Rabbi Rami Shapiro
5½ x 8½, 240 pp, Quality PB, 978-1-59473-109-9 **$16.99**
(A book from SkyLight Paths, Jewish Lights' sister imprint)

The Women's Haftarah Commentary
New Insights from Women Rabbis on the 54 Weekly Haftarah Portions, the 5 Megillot & Special Shabbatot
Edited by Rabbi Elyse Goldstein
Illuminates the historical significance of female portrayals in the Haftarah and the Five Megillot.
6 x 9, 560 pp, Quality PB, 978-1-58023-371-2 **$19.99**

The Women's Torah Commentary
New Insights from Women Rabbis on the 54 Weekly Torah Portions
Edited by Rabbi Elyse Goldstein
Over fifty women rabbis offer inspiring insights on the Torah, in a week-by-week format.
6 x 9, 496 pp, Quality PB, 978-1-58023-370-5 **$19.99**
HC, 978-1-58023-076-6 **$34.95**

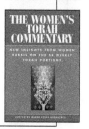

*A book from SkyLight Paths, Jewish Lights' sister imprint

About Jewish Lights

People of all faiths and backgrounds yearn for books that attract, engage, educate, and spiritually inspire.

Our principal goal is to stimulate thought and help all people learn about who the Jewish People are, where they come from, and what the future can be made to hold. While people of our diverse Jewish heritage are the primary audience, our books speak to people in the Christian world as well and will broaden their understanding of Judaism and the roots of their own faith.

We bring to you authors who are at the forefront of spiritual thought and experience. While each has something different to say, they all say it in a voice that you can hear.

Our books are designed to welcome you and then to engage, stimulate, and inspire. We judge our success not only by whether or not our books are beautiful and commercially successful, but by whether or not they make a difference in your life.

For your information and convenience, at the back of this book we have provided a list of other Jewish Lights books you might find interesting and useful. They cover all the categories of your life:

Bar/Bat Mitzvah	Life Cycle
Bible Study / Midrash	Meditation
Children's Books	Men's Interest
Congregation Resources	Parenting
Current Events / History	Prayer / Ritual /
Ecology / Environment	Sacred Practice
Fiction: Mystery, Science	Social Justice
Fiction	Spirituality
Grief / Healing	Theology / Philosophy
Holidays / Holy Days	Travel
Inspiration	Twelve Steps
Kabbalah / Mysticism / En-	Women's Interest
neagram	

Stuart M. Matlins, Publisher

Or phone, fax, mail or email to:
JEWISH LIGHTS Publishing
An imprint of Turner Publishing Company
4507 Charlotte Avenue • Suite 100 • Nashville, TN 37209
Tel: (615) 255-2265 • www.jewishlights.com
Prices subject to change.

Printed in the USA
CPSIA information can be obtained
at www.ICGtesting.com
JSHW052020140824
68134JS00027B/2572